To

....

From

....

Date

....

DEVOTIONS
from the BEACH

100 DEVOTIONS

THOMAS NELSON
Since 1798

Thomas Nelson titles may be purchased in bulk for educational, business, fund-raising, or sales promotional use. For information, please e-mail SpecialMarkets@ThomasNelson.com.

Unless otherwise noted, Scripture quotations are taken from the Holy Bible, New Living Translation. © 1996, 2004, 2007, 2013 by Tyndale House Foundation. Used by permission of Tyndale House Publishers, Inc., Carol Stream, Illinois 60188. All rights reserved.

Scripture quotations marked NKJV are from the New King James Version®. © 1982, 1992 by Thomas Nelson. Used by permission. All rights reserved.

Scripture quotations marked ESV are taken from The ESV® Bible (The Holy Bible, English Standard Version®), copyright © 2001 by Crossway, a publishing ministry of Good New Publishers. Used by permission. All rights reserved.

Scripture quotations marked NIV are from The Holy Bible, New International Version®, NIV®. Copyright © 1973, 1978, 1984, 2011 by Biblica, Inc.® Used by permission of Zondervan. All rights reserved worldwide. www.Zondervan.com. The "NIV" and "New International Version" are trademarks registered in the United States Patent and Trademark Office by Biblica, Inc.®

Scriptures quotations marked MSG are taken from THE MESSAGE, copyright © 1993, 1994, 1995, 1996, 2000, 2001, 2002 by Eugene H. Peterson. Used by permission of NavPress. All rights reserved. Represented by Tyndale House Publishers, Inc.

The devotions were written by Miriam Drennan and Betsy Painter.

ISBN 978-1-400-21190-6

Printed in China

20 21 22 23 WAI 6 5 4 3

CONTENTS

BREAKFAST ON THE BEACH

"Come and have some breakfast!" Jesus said.

JOHN 21:12

Following Jesus' death, several disciples got up early, took their fishing nets, tossed the nets in the water, and . . . nothing. Not a bite. Until a stranger onshore suggested they try fishing on the other side of the boat. Suddenly their nets were bulging, and they knew who had called to them. Jesus invited them to bring over some of their catch, then said, "Come and have some breakfast!"

It all seems so . . . normal! We create so much unnecessary hoopla. We plan, we implement, and we work hard, then we get frustrated when we get no results. Desperate and empty, we finally look to Jesus as a last resort–because we don't recognize who He is. And sometimes all He's asking is that we stop striving and come join Him, take part in what He's prepared and created. The rest will come.

So declutter your mind of plans, schedules, and to-do lists. Instead, look out upon the waves, wiggle your toes in the sand, absorb the sights, smells, and sounds, and enjoy the moment for what it is. Jesus' invitation is for you today: "Come." For now, put aside your busyness and just be present with Him.

Lord Jesus, I just want to be still and commune
with You in gratitude and love.

DRIFTWOOD

Stand firm in the faith. Be courageous. Be strong.

1 CORINTHIANS 16:13

Some driftwood–formed when trees or other large chunks of wood are swept away by the sea–never returns to shore. The waterlogged wood is often consumed by tiny organisms called talitrids and gribbles. Doesn't this sound like what happens when we are in a quandary of doubt? When we drift away from our faith, we may experience such turmoil that we feel as if we're being eaten from the inside out. What better way for the enemy to render us useless than to have us doubt our beliefs?

We may question if we were ever faithful. We might wonder if this Christian life is really worth it. Maybe God, or one of His people, let us down and we're angry. Or we drift because we're distracted by our new promotion, relationship, or hobby–and we neglect our faith.

Whatever your issue, don't drift. Stay faithful–stand firm. If you're hurting, stay hopeful. Ask God to shed light, provide clarity. If you're experiencing a season of blessings, don't forget the Provider. Make your way back to shore and into His loving arms. When you do, having been purified and renewed, your "knots" smoothed, you'll find your faith stronger than ever.

Lord, draw me closer to You. Refresh my faith
so I can face anything with confidence.

TREASURES BENEATH THE SAND

"Wherever your treasure is, there the desires of your heart will also be."

LUKE 12:34

Metal detecting is a curious hobby often on display at the beach. Some comb the beaches from the first peek of daylight to sunset, intent on discovering valuable treasure. It may be jewelry, old coins, or relics from sea battles or pirate ships.

Certainly Jesus taught about treasures in His parables: the lost coin (Luke 15:8–10), the treasure in the field (Matthew 13:44), and the pearl (vv. 45–46). Through these stories He is often asking if we value what God values. Do we use our resources accordingly? Are we passionate about searching for earthly rewards or heavenly ones? What are we willing to sacrifice to obtain eternal honors?

We carry a longing in our hearts that possessions cannot fulfill. Money and things are fun–they really are–but they cannot sustain our spirits. Still, we attempt to satisfy ourselves with things that are substandard and counterfeit while our spirits yearn for something much more mysterious and otherworldly.

Seeking God and His truths can be a balm to a scorched soul, bring peace to a troubled heart, and offer joy to a frazzled spirit. Let others pile up material possessions; guide your detector toward the less tangible but unspeakably more valuable prizes of spiritual comfort and wisdom.

Lord, give me a seeker's heart to discover Your truths,
and I will safeguard them as treasures in my heart.

FINAL RINSE

If we admit our sins. . . . He'll forgive our sins and purge us of all wrongdoing.

1 JOHN 1:9 MSG

Remember when, as a kid, you ran back from the beach, ravenous after a day of play? Perhaps you were headed to the car, a beach-house kitchen, or a hotel room. As you raced toward a meal, your mother called out to you, "Rinse off before you come in!"

Outdoor showers and spigots are commonplace at the beach, yet no matter how hard we try, we can never get truly clean using them. Sure, we can get a lot of sand off, but we still wind up tracking in countless gritty grains.

Whenever we meet with the Lord, whether we realize it or not, we are ravenous. Yet He does not demand that we wash off the sin we inevitably track in before we partake of time with Him. Thankfully, Jesus doesn't require the same degree of cleanliness our mothers did. And even if He did, no matter how hard or how long we tried, we would still be wearing our sin as we approached Him.

When Jesus washes us clean with His grace and forgiveness, He fills our spirits with His. From that moment on, we are clean and satisfied, but we will need to be cleansed another time. Whenever we run to Him, He receives and rinses us, reminding us that He has taken care of it all.

Lord Jesus, whenever I come to You wearing
my sin, please wash me clean.

THE STRENGTH OF SEA OATS

"Take my yoke upon you. . . . For my yoke is easy to
bear, and the burden I give you is light."

MATTHEW 11:29–30

*U*niola paniculata–sounds like a defense weapon, doesn't it? And it is. But
you know it better as lovely, graceful, waving-in-the-wind sea oats.

Picking sea oats is against the law in some states. Why is this grass so
important? Deep beneath the surface, the root system of these willowy grasses
is strong and complex–the kind of strength the sand and soil need to hold them
in place during a hurricane, a tropical storm, and other extreme weather conditions. Other benefits: this grass catches sand and forms dunes; by all accounts,
it is immune to pests; and once established, it is very low-maintenance. It can
withstand drought, and blowing sand actually stimulates its growth. And for
us, as we walk to the shore, the sea oats also indicate that we're almost to the sea.

When Jesus takes hold of our hearts, there is a similar effect. This gentle
Friend builds a root system that can withstand storms and extreme weather
conditions–and many of these situations actually stimulate our spiritual
growth. Jesus protects and builds us, He is immune to evil, and His "yoke is
easy" and His "burden . . . is light." And as we journey on, He tenderly reminds
us that we're almost there.

Lord, the sea oats illustrate how perfectly You crafted this
world and my spiritual life. I praise You for Your creation.

LET IT GO

He has removed our sins as far from us as the east is from the west.

PSALM 103:12

There's that moment when you're flat on your back, eyes closed, the warm sand conforming to your body . . . and you feel it, the release. It may take a few minutes, it may take a few days, but relaxation will eventually come.

When it happens, you're not aware of anything or anyone else around you. The collective sighs of waves and breeze invite you to synchronize, and you accept. Eventually you open your eyes, and their unfocused gaze absorbs the expanse that blankets your being–the sky, the horizon, the vastness of it all–without any interference.

We can liken this same open expanse to the true freedom we have by way of confessed sin–and how great is God's love for us. Taking our sins as far away as possible, He forgives, forgets, and washes us clean. We don't have this ability, but we can reap its eternal benefits.

So when that moment occurs, when all is released and you're enveloped by the vast sky and infinite horizon, capture it in your mind and embed it in your heart. Think about how many miles your eyes and thoughts can travel, and meditate on the fact that God's forgiveness reaches even farther, beyond anything you can imagine, and that His love is just as boundless.

Lord, Your forgiveness frees my soul from death and nurtures my spirit. Thank You for the vastness of Your mercy and love.

SINCERITY OF HEART

*"GOD judges persons differently than humans do. Men and
women look at the face; GOD looks into the heart."*

1 SAMUEL 16:7 MSG

If you've ever visited the Atlantic Ocean during the summer, you probably enjoyed its inviting warmth, spectacular color, and endless horizon. And if you've ever visited Antarctica (even if only in photographs), you probably experienced below-freezing temperatures, a colorless view, and an endless expanse of ice. These contrasting scenes make a point about God's people.

Some mature believers carry out the Lord's work without any fanfare. Even if they rarely discuss their faith, their work is their testimony. But sometimes their quietness makes their faith hard to read, and they seem a little unapproachable.

Other believers are very vocal about Jesus: they don't shy away from bringing Him up or quoting His Word. But sometimes these more verbal followers may seem intimidating because they're so sure of themselves.

God knows each human heart. The soft-spoken and the more vocal believer both have faith and gifts to share. And we need both types of believers in the world today.

We cannot judge another person's heart or the sincerity of his or her faith–and we don't need to! What's most important to remember is that penguins thrive in Antarctica while sea turtles flourish in the Atlantic–and both are essential members of earth's community.

*Lord, thank You for all the members of Your family,
whether they're subtle or outspoken. We all count.*

SUMMER SHOWER

A friend loves at all times.

PROVERBS 17:17 NKJV

It's not unusual for a shower to pop up on the beach, but it is an inconvenience. This isn't supposed to happen on your vacation–you're on borrowed time, after all! Can't the weather wait until you've pulled out of the parking lot? So inconvenient.

We often treat our friends with the same regard: *Oh, not again! Can't she wait? This is not a good time.* Let's be honest: If a dear friend phoned now, would you give your undivided attention? If she left a tearful message, would you call her back immediately? Would you quickly reassure her that you are available and supportive?

Maybe the issue she's dealing with seems simple to you; maybe you disapprove of her choices; maybe her life seems easy compared to yours. Still, you really have no excuse for not being there for her–not if she's your friend. And not if you are hers.

Remember, she knows you can't fix it for her. All she's asking for is just a bit of your time. You've probably inconvenienced her at some point too. Someday you will need her again, and just as with a summer shower, we don't always get to pick those days. Proverbs 17:17 instructs us to love our friends "at all times"–not just the ideal ones. Go ahead–call her.

Lord, give me ears that listen the way You do, and give me a heart to welcome an interruption when it involves a good friend.

TAKE THE HIGH ROAD

*Work at telling others the Good News, and fully carry
out the ministry God has given you.*

2 TIMOTHY 4:5

L isten to the sound your flip-flops make as sand swooshes in and out between your heels and the soles. Sometimes the sand feels nice as it glides through, but eventually it feels annoying. It's like the way we feel when we share the gospel–happy or slightly irritated.

We need to be mindful of two things when we share Christ with people and they do not accept Him. First, they rejected Jesus, not us; and second, it's possible they will return to Him later. We cannot "save" anyone, and we are not guaranteed that any part of our message will be well received. We're called just to deliver it.

You may ask, *But what if the one who rejects Him is a close friend or family member?* We can't exactly walk away, and we may endure a bit of hostility. Take the high road. Work to avoid any conflicts. We know that love covers a multitude of sins (1 Peter 4:8). So love him or her steadily. You have done your part–now let God do His. And whatever the response, whether you feel good or gritty, stay hopeful!

*Abba, Father, give me the words and actions that testify to Your
salvation. I can always deliver Your message, knowing that its
reception is up to You and up to the loved one I share with.*

FEEDING BIRDS

The Lord . . . satisfies your desires with good things so
that your youth is renewed like the eagle's.

PSALM 103:2,5 NIV

eagulls are as integral to the beach as rocks, sand, and waves. If you think about it, a beach without seagulls–which is indicative of treacherous weather–is a scary, lonely place. Their presence helps identify where you are and reinforces that conditions are at least tolerable.

But what happens when you feed seagulls? It's fun for a while, giving a crumb or two to those that dare approach . . . and then you're surrounded by all their friends. As their numbers grow larger, their demands grow louder, and soon you're swatting them away. You run–but they follow!

Insecurities are like seagulls. In a way, they identify where you are in your spiritual journey, and they reinforce your humanity. You consider entertaining one or two: You want to be part of the right crowd, so you consider sharing a juicy tidbit of gossip. You want to look like a trendsetter, so you mull over purchasing that purse you really can't afford. There's no harm in wanting to have friends or look good, right?

But what happens when you feed your insecurities? Do they fade away, or do they increase in number and become overwhelming? Feed seagulls as you wish, but starve those insecurities. They'll always demand more than you can bear to lose.

Lord, give me strength not to feed my insecurities.
Instead I ask You to feed my soul with good
things so it is satisfied and renewed.

BUOYED BY GRACE

God declared an end to sin's control over us by giving
his Son as a sacrifice for our sins.

ROMANS 8:3

They hold docks, secure nets, save people. Buoys of all kinds serve to lift up and support. We tend to overlook them except in times of need, such as inclement weather.

Consider a certain life-threatening situation: our struggle with sin. How often do we feel our sin is so hopeless that it's beyond the Lord's mercy? Whether it's an individual or collective sin, we feel resigned to the attitude that we cannot change.

We need a spiritual buoy to secure us. Without buoys, docks and boats float away and nets sink to the ocean floor. Without God, we suffer difficult consequences. So we have a choice: confess our sin or turn away from God in guilt. If we choose to succumb to guilt, we are suggesting that our sin is bigger than God's power. But Paul declared, "There is no condemnation for those who belong to Christ Jesus" (Romans 8:4). No sin or struggle is beyond God's forgiveness.

As you grow in grace, you realize that well-secured docks can stabilize boats, and well-secured nets don't sink–neither functions properly without buoys. God's grace holds us the same way, to keep us from destruction and discouragement. Let Him lift you up today.

Father, I recognize my sin and ask Your forgiveness.
Raise me from my guilt so I may praise You.

DOLPHINS SHOW THE WAY

*"The LORD will guide you continually, giving you water
when you are dry and restoring your strength."*

ISAIAH 58:11

Oh, they are so playful, leaping, jumping, talking to one another. Play is as important to dolphins as they are to one another. Dolphins are very social creatures, and they establish strong bonds. They care for one another, making sure any that are infirm stay fed and are taken to the surface to breathe. In fact, dolphins even extend this care and protection to other species, including whales and humans.

We know dolphins reflect God's creative design, and there are lessons we can take from them. Today's verse from Isaiah describes the results of personal acts of worship. Isaiah 58 instructs us to do those works that most please the Lord: free the oppressed, share food, shelter the homeless (vv. 6–7). In short, we should meet others' most pressing needs whatever the cost to ourselves. Then the Lord sustains us.

Remarkably, dolphins do this naturally, connecting and communicating and helping–even at their own risk. Sometimes, given their playful nature, we forget their bravery.

When we reach out with sincere, worshipful hearts to help meet others' needs, we receive God's blessing. Let us show the compassion of dolphins, and see the Lord guide us all our days.

*Lord, what magnificent creatures You made in
dolphins! How can I be more like them?*

YOU KNOW ENOUGH

Make it your goal to live a quiet life, minding your own business.

1 Thessalonians 4:11

Every girls' beach trip has a planner in the group; otherwise there would be no girls' beach trip. This person researches your rental options, makes reservations, scopes out area restaurants, checks the weather/tide reports down to the hour, and downloads coupons to various attractions.

Planners are truly helpful, but is it possible to have too much information? How many of us google new acquaintances to get some glimpses of their lives? Maybe we seek out the play-by-play on our neighbors' divorce. If we learn one person has been bad-mouthing another, why do we want to hear every syllable?

Whether we're reading too much into a relationship, seeking our own validation, or just being nosy, when we're this fascinated by information we are obsessed with other people's business.

Knowing facts is important. God gave us noggins to make smart decisions. But we create assumptions in our own minds, and not even our internet searches reveal the full story of any person's heart.

Can you let go of the incessant need to know everything and focus on your own business? Just take the beach trip and enjoy. You know enough!

Lord, I ask for Your help as I stop delving into others' lives. I trust You, Lord, that it is better for me to concentrate on my own.

A GREAT CALM

*He arose and rebuked the wind, and said to the sea, "Peace, be
still!" And the wind ceased and there was a great calm.*

MARK 4:39 NKJV

The sound of rolling waves lulls you into serenity. Minutes, even hours
may pass before you know it. To get that relaxed, you must be silent and
still. Then the waves can draw you into deeper silence, deeper stillness.

In an instant, however, this same environment can make you anxious.
Crashing waves and roaring surf indicate stormy conditions. Sometimes the
changes seem so random, you might wonder, *Who determines the state of the sea?*

Let's look at Scripture. In Mark 4, Jesus and His disciples were traveling
on a lake when a massive storm erupted. Waves and wind tossed the little boat.
How could a situation that was so peaceful one minute become so hazardous
the next? And through all that, Jesus slept!

Panicked, the disciples woke Jesus. He rose and simply told the storm to
stop. The point He made? As God's Son, He determined the state of the "sea,"
and He was aware of the storm, even though it didn't appear that way. They
needed to trust that He could handle the danger at hand.

When storms interrupt your calm, take to heart the Lord's command:
"Peace, be still!" As the waves settle, let Him draw you into your own "great
calm," into deeper silence, deeper stillness.

*Lord, You know about the squall in my spirit today. Will
You bring Your peace to the issue and to my heart?*

FOLLOW THOSE FOOTPRINTS

He is your example, and you must follow in his steps.

1 PETER 2:21

Go out on the beach early in the morning, and you'll likely find sets of tracks in the sand. They can be paw prints from a dog, claw prints from a bird, human footprints, or even some that are unidentifiable. The next time you see tracks, let your eyes follow them. Do they continue on straight, or do they meander? Are the impressions faint or bold? Farther down the beach, do the prints vanish?

Often we will follow others' whims, fancies, and trends. Over time, they meander and fade—and since we're following someone else's steps, they do not truly represent our own paths.

As you look at the sand, see if you can locate some footprints. Putting your feet inside them, follow wherever they lead. Is the stride larger than yours? Maybe you find yourself jumping from one footprint to the next! This is what it's like to try to follow the law of the Scriptures. The steps are so numerous and complicated, we soon grow exhausted. But then how will we attain righteousness? "Thank God!" Paul wrote. "The answer is in Jesus Christ our Lord" (Romans 7:25).

The law helps us recognize that we need a Savior. We need One whose steps are so large we can jump right into them. Jesus' righteousness provides for us as we follow Him. Don't follow any footsteps but His.

Lord, thank You for giving me a sure
path to You in Your Son, Jesus.

PACKING UP

"Make yourselves at home in my love."

JOHN 15:9 MSG

Do we have to leave?" "Can't we stay just a little longer?" Perhaps the saddest part about visiting a beach is leaving it. You pack up, you say your good-byes to friends, and you shake off the sand until the next visit.

Some of us depart in a flurry of activity, thinking that the quicker our departure, the fewer our heart pangs. Others of us linger hours after our scheduled departures, wanting one last look, one last hug, one last memory.

What kinds of good-byes happen in your prayer life?

Some days we race through, as though communion with our Creator were an item to check off our to-do lists. On other days all those voices vying for attention will just have to wait; we want to spend time with our Maker. We've reached our human limits, and we want nothing more than to be still in Him. So we remain as long as possible because of the peace, the comfort, and the rest we find in His presence.

When's the last time you had that sort of communion with the Lord? When you experience those moments, drink deeply. Welcome Jesus and stay with Him. As in any good conversation, give Him time to speak and yourself time to listen. When the day becomes busy, as it surely will, stay mindful that He remains with you—every minute. Unlike a vacation at the beach, this visit never has to end.

Lord, thank You for abiding with me even when my commitment to abide with You wanes. I want to be at home with You.

SHORELINE SURPRISES

He washed away our sins, giving us a new birth and new life through the Holy Spirit.

TITUS 3:5

The most interesting things can wash up on shore: remnants of a larger story we aren't privy to, evidence of a time that has passed, items that don't belong in the ocean but are now a part of the beach scene. A child's shoe that had washed out to sea; a fishing rod that slipped out of a boat; sunglasses that were jarred loose by a wave: these pieces of stories remind us that the sea has the final say on their destination and configuration.

In the same way, sin didn't belong in God's original landscape, nor was it intended for the human race. Nonetheless, it is now part of our reality. After being tossed about, our random sins wash ashore to lie in full view, and as we stroll by them we are forced to decide: Will we keep walking and leave them for someone else to clean up? Or maybe stomp them into the sand to disappear . . . for a while? Maybe we decide it's time to face our sin–pick it up and put it in the garbage once and for all.

Unless we let God wash our errors away, sin's stronghold will continue to ebb and flow in our lives, keeping us from truly experiencing the new life He's waiting to lavish on us. Fortunately, we can look forward to indescribable peace in knowing that the Lord (not the sea) has the final say on our sin's destination.

*Father, fill me with Your strength to put away
my sins once and for all. Help me fully realize
that they don't define my story anymore.*

VESSELS OF HONOR

If you keep yourself pure, you will be a special utensil for honorable use. . . .
You will be ready for the Master to use you for every good work.

2 TIMOTHY 2:21

Watch for a moment the various boats and ships as they glide past on the water. Some are massive, carrying cargo. Others may be sailboats and speedboats, commercial fishing boats, tour boats, even kayaks. Some gleam with newness and care, while others show wear. These boats may be made of any number of materials, like wood, fiberglass, or metal. No matter what type the vessel, its age, or its exterior, we don't know what's going on inside. We casual spectators can't see on board to know what's there.

Similarly, as people we too can sometimes hide menacing cargo and get away with it . . . for a while. At least long enough to do some damage. How, then, do we purge the pain and get cleansed so we can become special utensils honorable enough for the Lord to use?

According to Paul's instructions to Timothy, we must remove what's dishonorable in our lives. We should ask God to point out what needs to go, ask Him for strength to release it, and then do it. Only then can any of us be purified and become useful vessels of honor. Unlike the boats and ships we witness sailing the sea, we can always gleam with the Lord's special care.

Lord, fill my heart with Your truth and love so I can be a utensil
that honors You—in my words, in my works, in my daily walk.

THE LANGUAGE OF BELLS

The LORD God called to Adam and said to him, "Where are you?"

GENESIS 3:9 NKJV

S ome bells are large enough to be heard from great distances, alerting with intent. Other times you hear them as you wander along boat slips or harbors, as though the wind gently nudges them awake to announce your arrival.

Ship bells speak a particular language out on the water. Crews use them primarily for communicating through fog. The bells announce when the vessel is anchored or in trouble, or simply to make a boat's presence known.

Prayer gives us the same tool–but thankfully, our Creator is already in pursuit. Our prayers, we think, let God know how things are going, but in fact we announce nothing He is not already aware of. We actually pray to acknowledge God, petition Him, and commune with Him.

God pursues us whether we believe Him, believe in Him, or don't believe at all. He desires the connection; we, sometimes unknowingly, are starved for it. Our prayers then do not alert Him to our presence but rather alert us to His.

When we become disillusioned and trapped in a fog of confusion, we need to sound the alarm. With this in mind, remember that He is always looking for us, searching us out, just as He did Adam so long ago–no matter how lost we are. Whatever ship bells we ring in our prayers, we have a God who will find us, meet us, and carry us back into His light.

Lord, I cannot fathom the boundlessness of Your love and the reasons You pursue me. I am so thankful for Your love.

TIDE POOLS: A TIGHT FIT

Fearing people is a dangerous trap, but trusting the LORD means safety.

PROVERBS 29:25

Tide pools are wondrous things–little microcosms containing fascinating bits and pieces of life that are accessible to humans when the tide is out. Some of the animals that inhabit them are unable to roam on dry land, so during low tide they adapt to their smaller, more confined surroundings.

As women we can get trapped in any number of life's tide pools. Some of us go in willingly, but others of us fail to notice the tide ebbing away. Soccer season, school fund-raisers, career opportunities, fitness, friends, ministry: any one of these can take over our schedules and throw us off-center, to the detriment of other needs and activities. Often this happens because we're afraid to say no to yet another overwhelming commitment; we fear someone's reaction. So we agree, and we don't realize we've been snared until the tide is completely out.

What tide pools are you confined in? Let's not be afraid to pick and choose what "pools" we inhabit, and for how long. We shouldn't hesitate to set our own schedules and commitments. Is it time to crawl out of one pool (or several) and get back to experiencing the full scope of living God wants for you?

Father God, as I go about my commitments, please keep me from falling prey to intimidation. Remind me that You are the only One I answer to.

REFLECTIONS

Clothe yourselves with tenderhearted mercy, kindness,
humility, gentleness, and patience.

COLOSSIANS 3:12

In one shopping trip at the beach, we go from the window-gazing exclamation, "Oh! That is the cutest swimsuit! I wonder if they have it in my size" to dressing-room-mirror resignation. We've all twisted and turned under unflattering fluorescent lights, lamenting that the outfit looks so odd and dumpy on us. But the fact is, whatever your reflection is, it doesn't tell the whole story about you. Does it describe your kind heart, your faithfulness as a friend, your generosity toward people in need? Of course not!

That's the thing about reflections; we really need to look beyond the outer shell and go deeper into the soul. Instead we tend to grab hold of the first critical thought that comes to mind and issue judgment. At a glance a neighbor may appear grumpy and unapproachable, but after taking a longer look, you discover he suffers from arthritis and misses his deceased wife. When we don't look deeper, our judgment will be inaccurate.

When we consider that others are drawing the same conclusions based on our own outward appearances, we should be humbled. By taking time to understand why a person is the way he or she is and extending grace, we may also begin to unlock some grace for ourselves. Eventually this quality may emerge as a recognizable and welcome part of our own reflection!

Lord, help me give everyone—including myself—the
benefit of the doubt. Show me how to extend mercy,
again and again and again, just as You do.

COCONUTS AND YOU: ENDLESSLY USEFUL!

The vessel that he made of clay was marred in the hand of the potter; so he made it again into another vessel, as it seemed good to the potter to make.

JEREMIAH 18:4 NKJV

A familiar sight on tropical beaches, coconuts are a hot topic these days. Only a few facts seem certain about this controversial food item: First, many agree their meat is delicious, but experts disagree as to their health benefits. One sure thing about coconuts is that they don't last forever; once opened, they should be enjoyed quickly. And like many other natural products, coconuts can be used in seemingly countless ways that can affect millions of people.

This latter fact is also true of you. Your mind, heart, talents, physical abilities, even your limitations–God can put them to work on His behalf! Make an impact by funding clean water in a poor country. Be a friendly face behind a cash register or a trusted friend to a teenager. Your wise counsel can keep an innocent man from going to prison; your research can help identify a cure for a deadly disease. Every offering, when empowered by God, is significant and impactful.

The next time you see a coconut, consider the wonders and possibilities contained within. The next time you look in the mirror, do the same thing. Ask God to use every bit of you to accomplish His work. The steps may be small or large– but the impact may reverberate for generations.

Lord, what will You have me do? Show me some new ways to affect the people and world around me for good.

A STEADFAST LOVE

God created the great creatures of the sea and every living thing with
which the water teems. . . . And God saw that it was good.

GENESIS 1:21 NIV

And God saw that it was good." It sure is–especially when you have an oceanfront view!

Grasp that for a moment: the sea, the sand, the rocks, the crustaceans, the fish, the waves–God made every detail. Every molecule, every grain, shell, and gill–He created the entire scene you're taking in. And then He went even further: He gave us His Son, who provided a way for us to live forever.

You may be thinking, *That's true, and that's good, but right now I have daily realities to face. A lost job. A broken relationship. A failed endeavor. A missed opportunity. Yes, God has provided the way for us to have eternal life, but what about the groceries I need this week?*

From our vantage point, life can seem overwhelming and even out of control. But He who created the intricacies of the earth and its oceans loves us with a steadfast love (Lamentations 3:22). He proved this by giving us His Son. Have you surrendered your details to God to figure out? He's got a purpose-filled plan. We may not see the bigger picture as clearly as His oceanfront views, but we can trust that He sees it, and He is working it out. And we'll see that it too is good.

Lord, sometimes I forget that You see my needs, my
cares, my desires. Help me release any distrust and
doubt so I may fully know Your love and care.

A SCULPTURE IN SAND

All the Israelite men and women who were willing brought to the LORD freewill
offerings for all the work the LORD through Moses had commanded them to do.

EXODUS 35:29 NIV

Have you seen the elaborate sand sculptures some talented people build? The subjects range from tributes to classical works of art to favorite cartoon characters. The detail is amazing, and the way the sculptors embrace their medium is remarkable.

There are also those sweet little sand castles built with a child's plastic pail and shovel. The little handprints provide evidence that young artists have carefully patted and packed the sand.

In both cases, the sculptors reach a point of completion, satisfied they have done their best.

Today's Scripture refers to a different work of art: the tabernacle. If you read Exodus 35, you'll see the word *willing* multiple times—more often than the word *skilled*. In terms of service, is it more important to be willing or skilled?

The Lord is concerned that we always try our best. The quality of our work should reflect the abilities God has given us. We can't overlook, however, passion and willingness. Attitude and energy are just as important as the work itself.

For the Israelites, a combination of willingness and skillfulness built a tabernacle. Sand sculptors of all ages build castles. What are you building?

Lord, make me willing to build for You, and show
me what projects You have planned for me.

PELICANS: PRIVATE DINING

After the fire there was the sound of a gentle whisper.

1 KINGS 19:12

White pelicans, which winter along coasts, often eat collaboratively, sharing a school of fish. At other times, they may prefer to eat alone because other birds try to steal their food. These uninvited dinner guests will take every last morsel from their host, so it's no wonder white pelicans sometimes seek more private dining experiences.

Do you identify with the pelican? Does it seem as though uninvited "guests" just take and take, leaving you to starve mentally or emotionally? Maybe it's family, friends, work, church commitments, social engagements, or all of these. No one seems willing to step up and help, and you feel alone in the chaos.

Could some of the frustration be self-created? Elijah the prophet was irritated with God's people and afraid of the wicked queen Jezebel. He ran for his life, succumbing to fear and abandoning the faithful. If you're familiar with the story in 1 Kings 19, you know that God directed Elijah to stand in His presence. God then sent a windstorm, an earthquake, and a fire, but Elijah did not find God in the calamities. He found Him instead in the "gentle whisper" that followed. The voice directed Elijah to go back and enlist help.

God knew Elijah was worn-out, and He knows you are too. Listen for the still, small voice that may be telling you to find help. Then, like a white pelican, you can eat safely and stop starving.

Lord, please give me the strength to confront those who demand too much and the humility to enlist help as You direct.

GET TO THE GOOD PART

"Mary has chosen that good part, which will not be taken away from her."

LUKE 10:42 NKJV

What is it about the beach cookout that makes food taste better? The more impromptu, the better. People bring what they have, and new friends are made. We eat; we play. Eventually we gather round the fire and watch the flames until embers close down a lovely day.

Would we dare entertain so spontaneously at home? Or do we wait and plan for the perfect moment, the perfect time, and the perfect setting to create some wow factor?

In this age of tablescapes and celebrity chefs, we can easily lose sight of hospitality's purpose. As we can see from Luke 10:38–42, this happened even in biblical times. Martha was "worried and upset" trying to plan dinner for Jesus (v. 41). She wanted to present her best efforts, pull out all the stops; wouldn't we do the same if we knew He were coming?

But Jesus is in our homes every day; we're so busy with our tasks that many days we also miss "that good part." And when we invite others into our homes, we're so busy making sure everything is flawless we miss "that good part" with them too.

Think back to how satisfying that beach cookout feels. Invite a friend over for morning coffee instead of brunch. Or let the laundry wait so you can spend more time in prayer. Sometimes we have to peel away the trappings to get to "that good part."

Lord, help me be more spontaneous about how I invest
in the lives of others, and how I spend time with You.

MESSAGES IN SAND

"Neither do I condemn you," Jesus declared. "Go now and leave your life of sin."

JOHN 8:11 NIV

It's fun to write messages in the sand; it can also be cathartic. Some people take photos of their messages to send to friends; others may stand and watch as the waves wash the message away, leaving the sand completely smooth.

A woman caught in adultery was brought to Jesus. The Pharisees reminded Jesus that according to Moses' law, she should be stoned, and they awaited His response. Not once but twice, Jesus stooped and wrote on the ground with His finger. We shouldn't miss what Jesus said between His writings, but what words or images did He finger into the sand?

Some believe that He wrote the Pharisees' names and their sins. They cite Jeremiah 17:13: "Those who depart from Me shall be written in the earth, because they have forsaken the LORD, the fountain of living waters" (NKJV). In the preceding chapter from John, Jesus spoke of Himself as "living water" (John 7:38). Perhaps He was fulfilling a prophecy.

We don't know for sure, nor do we know who saw His message. It's possible, however, that once the crowd had dispersed and He was left to deal with the woman Himself, He'd written only one word: *forgiven*. And whether that message was erased by Him or the wind, her sins were also wiped away. Remember—so are yours.

Lord Jesus, by Your blood and resurrection, You provided a way for my sins to be erased. Thank You for this gift.

STUCK IN THE MUD

The Sovereign LORD is my strength; he makes my feet like the
feet of a deer, he enables me to tread on the heights.

HABAKKUK 3:19 NIV

It has a special texture and odor, and it's familiar mostly to South Carolina natives. It isn't quicksand, though for the many shoes lost, there is little difference–they suffer the same fate in the suction.

Plough mud is incredibly soft. If you happen to step in it, you're stuck. You'll slosh along, slower and slower, each step sucking your feet or shoes deeper. You'll hear its sighs and gasps as you pull and strain to keep moving.

Our faith can get like that too. Sometimes we simply get stuck. We're convinced a black cloud follows us around. Our lives feel stalled. We are alone in this big, lonely world while everyone else has direction. Even if their direction isn't one we'd choose, at least they're moving. We're just sitting and waiting in the mud. Where is God?

He is working, of course. Trees look positively lifeless in the winter, then bud in the spring, right? When you're stuck, stalled, or stale, stay faithful. Keep believing. Pray honestly and earnestly. Trust your joy will return. God has plans that will not leave you stuck in the mud. As today's verse says, the sovereign Lord will eventually give you "the feet of a deer" to get on higher, stabler ground–far above the mud.

Lord, I renew my belief that You are at work. If the tree
buds return in the spring, my faith will dislodge from
the mud and burst through with new growth too.

TIES THAT BIND

Even youths grow tired and weary . . . but those who
hope in the LORD will renew their strength.

ISAIAH 40:30–31 NIV

ander by an old dock or boat slips, and you'll hear the rhythmic moans of ropes. Whether they're holding a boat or serving as a safety railing, ropes cannot deviate from their purpose without devastating consequences. Their rest is reserved for another time.

Study those ropes. Time and tension contribute to their frayed, discolored appearance. Ironically, however, these seeming blemishes make them more pliable, more useful, and even stronger.

Do you experience similar stretching? You are quietly straining, moaning, painfully trying to keep it together for others' sake. You bear the marks of time and experience but don't seem to gain wisdom and strength. Quite often our pain has purpose; but just as often, we don't see it. Instead, we focus on the fear of what might happen if our grip should slip.

The fact is that even if we let go, God won't let go of us. Sometimes we can't hang on with our own strength. Then we have a choice: cling tightly, so fearful that we snap, or yield to God what we can't hold on to ourselves.

As with rope, time always imparts strengthening experience. As God does with all His children, He never drops them, no matter what they do.

Father, make my heart and spirit pliable enough
to receive Your divine instruction and faith.

ESCAPE THE EBB TIDE

In your unfailing love, O God, answer my prayer with your sure salvation.

PSALM 69:13

*E*bb tide describes the outgoing tide–the period between high tide and low. As women, we may find that our ebb tides can be almost worse than our low tides: that stumbling forward, receding, that feeling of helplessness. An ebb tide is a period of decline. It might be late notices on bills you cannot pay. The husband who seems distant. The announcement confirming layoffs are pending. We cannot get resolution, and we don't know whether to move forward or sideways. We're caught.

Sometimes these events unfold because of our bad decisions. Sometimes they have nothing to do with us. Regardless, we realize we are not in control–and we never were.

Psalm 69 shows David in a similar place. "Exhausted from crying for help," he couldn't "find a foothold" while "waiting for [his] God to help" (vv. 2–3). He suffered from ridicule and scorn. Whispers about his activities abounded, with added embellishment. But he waited and stayed faithful, knowing God's "sure salvation" would come.

When you find yourself being swept into the ebb tide, remember David's prayer. Trust God's timing and the provision that will come. And remember, the tide will rise again to take you safely back to shore.

Father, thank You for David's reminder to call out to
You in seemingly hopeless situations. Let me not forget
to praise You in times of both plenty and lack.

BEAUTIFUL BITS

*[Christ] had designs on us for glorious living, part of the overall
purpose he is working out in everything and everyone.*

EPHESIANS 1:11–12 MSG

People search for sea glass for different reasons: to make jewelry or art, to provide an activity for a restless child, or as collectors to gather the beautiful bits. Just think: these treasures start as broken, discarded glass, pieces of a former whole that no longer serve their intended purpose. Cast away, tossed about, taking some hard knocks, and finally emerging smooth, refined, beautiful: these pieces of glass are pursued by people with a new purpose in mind.

Likewise, we all have those days or seasons when we feel fragmented and useless, discarded and forgotten. Friends don't return calls, promotions pass us by, children take us for granted. Parts of a former whole, we find ourselves tossed about, taking hard knocks, unsure of our direction or purpose.

All the while, however, we are being pursued by One who has a new purpose in mind.

The Father knows and orchestrates our seasons of refinement–they are part of a greater plan. These seasons are not necessarily enjoyable, but throughout the tossing we can be sure we have a Father who loves us and establishes a purpose for us. Trust that during these seasons you are being refined and transformed into something that, like sea glass, is both useful and beautiful.

*Lord, renew my trust that You are always at
work, even when I can't see or feel it.*

LEANING TOWARD LIGHT

*"I am the light of the world. If you follow me, you won't have to walk
in darkness, because you will have the light that leads to life."*

Have you ever noticed how a palm tree's trunk curves and leans? Many appear to droop toward the ocean, but they're not seeking nourishment from the water. They're actually leaning toward another life source: the light the water reflects. The scientific term for this is *phototropism*. Interestingly, leaning this way makes it easier for them to reproduce successfully, since the current can carry their seeds away for dispersal.

This concept has *gospel* written all over it! Our spiritual depth and breadth as believers follow a similar course: we are seeds planted by a current of fellow believers who reflect light and help us grow. As we grow, we lean toward (or on) this same community to, in fact, reach for more of our true life Source: the Light of the world. And in His timing, our own seeds are planted and carried to other places to renew the process.

The light itself is essential for the one tree's survival; seed dispersal is essential for the survival of its species. For what reasons do you need to lean toward the Light today?

*Lord Jesus, thank You for the graceful reminder of who
You are, who I am, and what I need to do, so artfully
depicted in the lovely image of a palm tree.*

GLORY IN THE STARS

God's glory is on tour in the skies, God-craft on exhibit across the horizon.

PSALM 19:1 MSG

Have you ever wandered down the beach on a clear night? Did you lie down, stretch out on your back, and stare into the enormity of the sky? Whether you view them from the beach or somewhere else, stars are so vast it's easy to lose yourself in looking at them.

David wrote about this idea in Psalm 19, which opens, "The heavens declare the glory of God" (v. 1 NKJV). God reveals Himself to us in any number of ways, but in nature we see His power and creativity. The stars have been there throughout history, provided by God as "signs to mark sacred times, and days and years" and to "give light on the earth" (Genesis 1:14–15 NIV). The arrangement of the stars is not random. Over the centuries, they have helped sailors and awed scientists with their order. In addition to their many uses to us on earth, the stars exist also to declare God's glory. Are we, another of His creations, playing our part to display His glory?

On a night bright with the lights of heaven, take some time beside the lapping waves to admire God's handiwork. The stars have been here almost from the beginning, and they will remain after we're gone. In the meantime, they bear witness to God's glory. In the meantime, so should we.

Father, what a beautiful display for those of us who take the time to look! Thank You for the reminder the stars give me to declare Your glory.

BETTER BOAT SHOES

May the God of all grace . . . perfect, establish, strengthen, and settle you.

1 Peter 5:10 NKJV

S ome things just work better once they're broken in, and boat shoes are a prime example. Whether the shoes are canvas or leather, their rubber soles have a pattern cut into the bottom that gives the wearer extra grip on a wet deck. The leather ones, once rubbed with oil, repel water. Sailing enthusiasts will tell you, when these shoes are salt-logged and floppy, they function more effectively and are far more comfortable.

Friend, we need to take a cue.

How exciting it is when we become Christians! In the newness of it all, we explode with joy as we plan to save the world just as we've been saved and become experts in all things biblical and holy. That enthusiasm is great—but as brand-new believers we're often squeaky, and we rub people the wrong way. Oh, we've got the right idea about helping others find Jesus—but we're not broken in; we're not as effective as we can be. Yet.

Hardships, mentors, good times, biblical knowledge: all of these will contribute valuable learning and experience to make us salt-logged and floppy. Then we'll be truly useful for the kingdom.

If you're newly acquainted with Jesus, take care not to wear people out as you're getting broken in. Stay humble about all you have yet to learn; give that shoe time to loosen up! The results will be worth it.

Father God, teach me how to be effective for Your kingdom.

PENGUIN PECULIARITIES

He will restore, support, and strengthen you, and
he will place you on a firm foundation.

1 PETER 5:10

We can learn important lessons from the creatures that live on or near beaches, including various species of penguins. Compare, for instance, their on-land abilities and their water skills. On land, penguins have fewer predators and are generally unafraid of humans. On land, penguins move slowly, with a distinct and silly waddle. In the water, however, penguins can "fly" more than twenty miles per hour. On land, penguins are quite nearsighted, but their vision in the water is keen and clear.

In the water, these cartoonish birds transform from nearsighted and sluggish to sharp-eyed and fast. So why don't they simply remain in the water? Penguins are immersed for about 75 percent of their lives, but the beaches are key to their survival. You see, these birds have rookeries on shore where they breed, rest, and sometimes feed.

When we seek and find our God-ordained work, He gives us both great vision and the ability to soar. But during other seasons, we feel as if we're waddling across a barren space. If we take a cue from our penguin friends, at these times we should seek counsel and comfort from others, rest, and attend to other important matters. When it's time to soar again, the apostle Peter reminds us that God will renew us and restore us.

Father, when my life seems slow and uncertain,
remind me that this season is necessary. Show
me how to regroup and reconnect with You.

THE HAVEN OF HAMMOCKS

You were all called to travel on the same road and in the same direction, so stay together, both outwardly and inwardly.

Ephesians 4:4 msg

Hopefully your beach campsite or house has a hammock. Why are they so popular? That gentle rocking motion takes you back to infancy, when you were cradled in safety. The fibers that make up the hammock are so tightly wound you never fear their breaking, and within them you enjoy a unique kind of relaxation.

In contrast to the productive unity we see in the hammock's construction, we have the body of Christ. Often we believers disagree on everything from worship styles to biblical interpretation. Differing opinions aren't strange–we're not mass-produced. But when they block pursuing our shared purpose of reaching others for Christ, we've got a problem.

Somehow we have to bridge the gaps of our disagreements and find a way to bind ourselves together, like the fibers of a hammock, if we as a body are to be effective. Paul referred to it more eloquently as "endeavoring to keep the unity of the Spirit in the bond of peace" (v. 3 nkjv).

When the "endeavoring" actually occurs, seekers are enticed. Paying careful attention to the tight connections between believers, they will see the group's strength and feel cradled in the security of a body that rocks steadily.

Whether in the beach hammock or within your community of believers, enjoy the safety and comfort of good ties.

Father, show me how to love those who disagree with me. Bind us together in a unity that serves You well.

HEARTS AND OYSTERS

Take hold of my words with all your heart.

PROVERBS 4:4 NIV

Fresh oysters are a big treat–but you have to work at them a little. They're sharp-shelled and not easy to open. You carefully guide the knife tip to pierce, then wiggle into the hinge. When you hear a little pop, you slide in the blade, careful not to slice the oyster inside. You essentially pry oysters open at your own risk. But how lovely to discover what's inside!

Our hearts are much like oyster shells, particularly if we've experienced great pain or loss. The shell protecting a wounded heart remains sealed and sharp, protecting the fragile softness inside. We sometimes close our hearts even to God. Consider that out of all the places in the world He could reside, He desires our hearts! We're kidding ourselves to think we can truly keep Him away. We're able to shut Him out only because He allows us to.

Incidentally, a beautiful pearl forms when an irritant slips within the mantle folds of an oyster shell. Consider what treasures God may create if He has the same access to your heart!

Lord, thank You for being willing to enter even a heart as hard as mine, to dwell there and build.

THE PERFECT BEACH TRIP

To enjoy your work and accept your lot in life—this is indeed a gift from God.

ECCLESIASTES 5:19

When you hear the term *perfect beach trip*, what comes to mind? Can you think of a time when *everything* went as you hoped, or do you replay the foibles that occurred instead? *Well, there was that time it rained. Or the time we got lost for two hours trying to find the new beach house. Or the time our toddler got an ear infection the first full day we were there.* Hmm. Maybe at the point-by-point level, you've never had a perfect beach trip.

Sometimes we just want–even demand–perfection in order to enjoy our plans. The moment has to be exactly right, or we give up because it's utterly ruined. To be fair, planning and preparation are important. But if we spend our time waiting or hoping for perfect conditions and outcomes, we're wasting our time. Waiting for perfection leads to barren outcomes. As Ecclesiastes says, "Farmers who wait for perfect weather never plant. If they watch every cloud, they never harvest" (11:4).

Instead, why don't we learn how to react when imperfections inevitably occur? The writer of Ecclesiastes encourages us to "accept [our] lot in life." The next time your beach trip goes south, how can you make the most of the situation? What could you do to keep frustration from ruining the trip? How can you find the "gift from God" by rolling with the punches?

Lord, grant me a willingness to accept imperfection. Help me make this beach trip the best it can be, whatever happens.

RIP CURRENTS: DANGER AHEAD

*My life is worth nothing to me unless I use it for finishing
the work assigned me by the Lord Jesus.*

ACTS 20:24

Rip currents occur when water trapped between an underwater sand bar and the shore gives way and pushes back out to sea. Swimmers caught in these currents are cautioned to ignore their natural inclination to try to swim straight back to shore. Instead they should swim parallel to the shore to escape the current, then head back to safety.

In Acts 22 Paul was caught in a verbal rip current. He'd been attacked for blasphemy and defiling the temple with Gentiles. A Roman commander saw the uproar and arrested Paul, which ironically saved Paul from angry Jews. Now what?

Paul spoke Greek to the commander, indicating he was both well educated and well versed in the culture. This paved the way for him to address the crowd in Hebrew to let them know he was a devout Jew. And when he identified himself as a Roman citizen, Paul saw his life spared again.

Navigating the enemy "rip currents" as he did, Paul swam parallel with the shore: he spoke their languages, he reminded them of what they stood for, and he found common ground from which he could deliver his message.

How do you handle the rip currents of those who do not believe? Paul risked his very life among those who opposed him. Do you share his determination to serve Jesus?

*Lord Jesus, give me courage to venture out and handle the
rip currents in life, with the wisdom and words You provide.*

THE NOT-SO-HUMBLE HERMIT CRAB

Our purpose is to please God, not people. He alone
examines the motives of our hearts.

1 THESSALONIANS 2:4

If you put an empty seashell on a beach and a hermit crab spots it, the crab will move in, and another will move into its abandoned shell. If crabs had human feelings, we'd say perhaps the second crab envied what the other had all along and just waited to take advantage of an opening. Do you have friends–or frenemies–like that?

Maybe you were recognized at work for solving a problem only to have your supervisor accuse you of trying to take his or her job. Or perhaps someone gave you a backhanded compliment. Flattery coupled with envy is a dangerous combination.

The apostle Paul was accused of flattering his audience in Thessalonica. But as he ministered, he did not seek people's admiration, nor did he seek special treatment because he was an apostle (1 Thessalonians 2:6–8). Paul gave little attention to gushing. He never believed his own hype, and he trusted God with the rest.

There are people who want what you have: your job, your lifestyle, even your faith. Keep an eye out for the hermit crabs who wait to take over; be like Paul and humbly serve the God who gives you everything you have.

Father, You give me value—and no one
else can add to it or diminish it.

MYSTERIES AND MIRACLES

The LORD your God, the great and awesome God, is among you.

DEUTERONOMY 7:21 NKJV

Many beaches have some sort of mystery or spooky story attached to them. At most every coast, locals and fishermen have a strange tale that's part of the beach's folklore.

Too often we view God as a sort of ghost story. We love hearing tall tales that give us goose bumps, yet we yawn at the beautiful mysteries and miracles of God–accounts that reveal His character and set forth truth and promises for each one of us. How real is God to you?

When we refuse to engage Him, to devote time to meditate on His truths, our God diminishes into folklore–a warm presence we like to have around, but not a dynamic personality who changes everything!

We need God. He is not a legend or a nice story or even a scary story! He is our Creator who knows us intimately and wants us to know Him in the same way. God is not the protagonist in a charming old beach tale. Nor is He waiting to zap us with a stun gun if we don't go through the proper religious motions. Our God is alive. He is powerful, He is present, and He wants us to believe in all His mysteries and miracles.

Lord, let me feel Your presence, hear Your voice,
taste Your goodness. I believe in You!

THE PATH LESS TAKEN

An angel of the Lord spoke to Philip, saying, "Arise and go toward the south along the road which goes down from Jerusalem to Gaza." This is desert.

ACTS 8:26 NKJV

Coastal friends always know of a local path to the beach. You may walk over wooden planks instead of pristine boardwalks, but once you've arrived, you're at a prime beach location. It's the spot barely dotted with locals rather than filled with rows of tourists who pack in at a public entrance.

Crowds were packing in to hear Philip preach and see him perform miracles. Then God sent word to Philip to hit the desert road. He must have wondered why, but in this case, we know the answer: God wanted Philip to share the gospel in an encounter with an Ethiopian official.

Following Jesus involves taking a less-populated path. Sometimes this trail is not well-defined, so you find that your steps are more hopeful than sure. It may even be in a place others typically avoid–like the desert. But the path less taken has its advantages. You get to view God's creation as wild and free, not safe and manicured. Without all the noise, you hear His voice more easily. You're not fighting crowds who have chosen an easier, more obvious route. No, this path gives you quiet solitude.

And you learn that, if you must, you can travel this path alone. Because if you know who is leading you, you know you're safe in His hands.

Lord, today I choose Your path. Yours
is the only way to eternal life.

GET REAL

"What do you benefit if you gain the whole world but lose your own soul?"

MARK 8:36

Leafy sea dragons look like sea horses that have sprouted leaves. This appearance protects them from would-be predators. The sea dragons can also change colors to further camouflage themselves.

The sea dragon's life is spent fitting in, even disguising itself. Too often we think the same is true for us–that we need to focus on blending into the crowd, even disguising ourselves. Whatever group of people we're pursuing–the popular neighbors, the fashionable women, or the inner circle at church–we scheme about how to be in their presence. We study their habits and strategize how to make them accept us. It's hard work, trying to be something we're not.

We won't fit in long if the group's activities and values run counter to ours. Eventually we'll have to decide: Do we add more camouflage, or do we reveal what our beliefs and standards are?

It's a risk, being the people God created and intends us to be. But genuine peace comes only when we live out our faith as authentically as possible. As the psalmist declared, "I would rather be a doorkeeper in the house of my God than dwell in the tents of the wicked" (Psalm 84:10 NIV).

The next time you find yourself considering another layer of disguise, give a thought to the leafy sea dragons, who must hide in order to survive. They don't have a choice, but you do.

Father, reveal to me those people who belong to You,
people who will encourage and edify me. Give me the
courage to show my true colors, to Your glory.

RESCUE REQUIRED

I will sacrifice to You with the voice of thanksgiving. . . . Salvation is of the LORD.

JONAH 2:9 NKJV

When the lifeguard's whistle blows, an ambulance arrives, beach patrol shouts through a bullhorn, and leisurely tourists become pensive onlookers–something has happened. Someone got caught in a riptide or was injured, and the situation is precarious.

This was Jonah's predicament: he was in a deeply dangerous situation. He'd been running from God and found himself in the belly of a fish. He could not save himself. Many times the Lord walks through the fires and waves with us, but there are times He simply plucks us out of a situation–perhaps one we are either unwilling or unable to leave ourselves–and rescues us.

Some rescues take longer to occur. Sometimes our hearts are broken in the process: we're asked to leave a job or home we love. And the longer we cling to what we know–the unknown is so scary, after all–the more painful and difficult the rescue effort becomes. Taking a cue from Jonah's story, we might need to be rescued from a situation right now. There will be time for questions later.

Jonah made the astounding choice to praise God while still in the fish's innards. He acknowledged that "salvation is of the LORD," and God rescued him. When we're waiting for rescue, we can ask God (the ultimate Lifeguard) to show us what He's doing. But more important is our mimicking Jonah: praise God now with a full heart, and trust His response.

Lord, help me grow in my trust that You have rescued me from something I may never have to know about or understand.

NOTHING LEFT UNDONE

*"I do not pray for these alone, but also for those who
will believe in Me through their word."*

JOHN 17:20 NKJV

Long ago the sun was setting, but Jesus' work was not done. There was so much He needed to say–and He had to move quickly. But as He taught His brothers, evening settled in and He was not finished. There was another with whom He needed to speak.

As Jesus moved to the garden that night to pray over a multitude of things, He knew what He was facing; yet most of His prayer was devoted to those believers who would follow–in the coming days, years, and centuries. Here was a Man facing death, whose main concern was for those who'd never dined with Him, walked with Him, or even believed in Him. That night Jesus prayed for you and me. A short time later, His work would be complete. For us all.

What sorts of things do we do in a day? Laundry, grocery shopping, preparing meals. Away from the beach, if we're just visiting there, we pay bills, make appointments, finish a big project, plant a garden. In the process of completing our tasks, do we miss Jesus in the activities of our day? Do we miss the One who did not let His day, or His life, end without praying for us?

As you watch tonight's sunset, think about that night two thousand years ago. Have you left anything essential undone today?

*Lord, out of gratitude and love I come to You now.
Give me patience to leave unnecessary things
undone so that I may spend more time with You.*

LIGHTHOUSES

Though I sit in darkness, the LORD will be my light.

MICAH 7:8 NIV

They are mysterious, solitary, and majestic. Lighthouses serve a common purpose: to identify treacherous terrain and cut through fog and darkness, enabling safe passage for those who heed their warning.

Our Lord desires to be the same sort of beacon in our lives, but sometimes that can leave us feeling lonely. The prophet Micah must have felt very alone at times. God sent him to identify the infections of worldly interests occurring in Israel and warn the people what the consequences would be. As you can imagine, this message didn't make Micah a popular guy.

Here was this fellow telling people their religion was polluted. But they must have responded that Israel was getting rich and fat–this must have meant that God approved of what they were doing. So why listen to the prophet?

But just as the view from the top of a lighthouse is much broader than that from the beach, God's omniscient perspective was very different from Israel's. We know what happened to Israel–the predicted exile–but we don't know what happened to Micah. We do know that he was willing to sit in the dark, alone, and wait on God. How long did he wait? Did he have moments of despair? We certainly do.

Consider the ship that disregards a lighthouse: the ship will make progress for a while, but ultimately it hastens its own destruction. In times of uncertainty, wait on God. The light will come.

*Lord, give me Your strength. Send me Your
light as my trust in Your timing grows.*

WATER, WATER EVERYWHERE

"If you knew the gift of God, and who it is who says to you, 'Give Me a drink,'
you would have asked Him, and He would have given you living water."

JOHN 4:10 NKJV

It's interesting that while we're surrounded by water at the beach, it's not drinkable. It's beautiful, it's soothing, it's refreshing to splash in, but it will not give our bodies the necessary fluid we need each day.

God, who made our physical bodies to require water, also made the spiritual parts of us that live on beyond the physical. So it's no wonder we need "living water" as well. Why do so many of us remain parched?

Though God is our authentic Source for living water, we often look elsewhere. We'd rather splash around in the supplemental than quench our thirst with the fresh flow of living water.

In John 4 Jesus described living water to a woman who thought He meant she would not need to return to the well each day, which would have made life easier for her (v. 15). While following Christ doesn't guarantee an easy life, constant refills of living water give us perspective and strength to endure it–and even to authentically enjoy it.

Look around the beach today. Give a thirsty person a bottle of water from your stash. Observe the satisfied smile as his or her thirst is quenched. Our spirits have the same opportunity–and we are free to drink as often as needed.

Lord, let me receive Your living water and genuine refreshment.

LEAVE IT TO THE PROS

O LORD, do not stay far away! You are my strength; come quickly to my aid!

PSALM 22:19

Beach lifeguards must undergo a considerable amount of training. Their responsibilities extend beyond supervising beachgoers to include giving first aid, performing CPR, and rescuing stranded or injured swimmers. They make every effort to keep the environment safe and enjoyable.

Sometimes we attempt to be lifeguards to our friends. We want to call back those who stray, save those slipping into danger, and spend all our strength to keep them free from harm. It's a noble quest, but without proper boundaries, we can easily become someone's personal safety monitor—to his or her detriment.

Before you become too focused on one person's needs, ask yourself: *Why is this person important to me? Do I truly feel called to help her? Am I trying to do what only a professional should do?*

We need to help when we can but know when we're in too deep, such as when we get emotionally drained by someone's needs. Sometimes the best way to support a person is to step back and point him or her toward people more qualified to help.

Let's leave lifeguarding to those who are called and equipped. And rest assured that when you're off duty, the Lord will always "come quickly" to save those He loves.

Lord, enable me to gently release the people I'm not qualified to help into Your and others' care.

STORMS

The LORD said to Moses, "Why are you crying out
to me? Tell the people to get moving!"

EXODUS 14:15

When a severe storm is forecast, people gather sandbags, assemble disaster kits, secure boats, and plan evacuations. Believers and nonbelievers alike take steps to avoid disaster and keep people and pets safe. So why, when trouble strikes at home, do we shrug and say, "All I can do is pray"?

Consider the Israelites. Even as they were triumphantly escaping Egypt's tyranny, they could see Pharaoh and his army approaching, and they feared certain annihilation. Moses initially told them they needed only to be still (v. 13)—but God had a different response: "Tell the people to get moving!"

Yes, there are times when we need to be still, pray, and wait for Him. But too often prayer is an excuse for a delayed reaction or not doing anything at all. At times God wants us to get involved because quite often He reveals His power in those situations.

Whatever the storm that threatens—a calamity in the family, illness, a sudden job loss, a financial challenge—God may be impressing more than prayer on your heart. He may be summoning you to take action. If that's the case, trust that He will equip you. You may not part the Red Sea, as Moses did, but be assured you are doing your part to safeguard those you love.

Father God, show me how to respond to the storm
at hand, leaning on Your power, not my own.

PEBBLE BEACHES

The LORD directs the steps of the godly. He delights in every detail of their lives.

PSALM 37:23

The appearance of a pebble beach can be misleading. Made up of little stones and other coarse materials, it looks forbidding. This isn't like the warm, soft, sandy beaches we're used to. So how do we navigate comfortably through this rough-looking terrain?

When we actually touch the pebbles, we realize the stones are smooth and can be quite slippery. Perhaps we don't move as swiftly as we do on hard sand; perhaps it's not as squishy as dry sand, but we can definitely walk on this surface–even with bare feet.

We anticipate events in our lives the same way. We dread performance reviews, report cards, medical test results; we delay difficult conversations with loved ones; we prepare to be defensive with customer service. We get hyped up about situations and conversations, just knowing they're going to be awful.

This thought process is defeating. We assume we already know the outcome, as though we can read minds and predict the future. If God directs our steps, however, we need to trust Him with our walk.

Before building a crisis in your head, stop the rush of thoughts and pray– for peace, for wisdom, and for words. Ask God to calm your anxiety and guide you. And even if you aren't completely sure what will happen, just take off your shoes and walk over the pebbly beach–with Him. It's the only way to get to the next destination.

Father, let me draw upon Your wisdom so I will know how to face every situation. Thank You for staying so close to me.

TURTLE TOGETHERNESS

"Whoever does the will of God is My brother and My sister and mother."

MARK 3:35 NKJV

Perhaps you've heard of the turtle walks that take place in several coastal states in America and on foreign beaches as well. Turtle conservationists or wildlife specialists lead groups on a search for nesting females so they may witness the laying of eggs.

You may be surprised to learn that once the females lay their eggs, they return to the water. The eggs are left alone, incubating for about forty-five to seventy days, then hatch. From there, the hatchlings work their way together into the sea.

Such natural companionship may feel unnatural to you, particularly if you were an only child, grew up in a less-than-happy family, or are no longer in touch with your family of origin. Maybe you felt emotionally or physically abandoned, which has left you with scars and an endless longing for close friends or a new family.

Healing begins and ends at the cross. As today's Scripture indicates, believers are members of a spiritual, eternal family who, when living in accordance with God's will, can provide healthy support and the encouragement you need.

Just like the baby turtles, those in your community will stay close to you and grow with you—and your healing can begin.

Father, please help me find my community, and help me reach out to others who are in the same situation I'm in.

BEACH PLAY

This day is holy to our Lord. Do not sorrow, for the joy of the LORD is your strength.

NEHEMIAH 8:10 NKJV

Have you ever watched dogs and children at play on the beach? They are unleashed, unhindered, and ready to drink in all that the expanse has to offer. They run, jump, and cavort, more raucous than usual–not to draw attention to themselves, but rather out of the excitement they feel at having a large play area and freedom to let loose.

In contrast, the Israelites in Nehemiah 8 were mournful, having squarely faced how far they'd strayed from God's law. As they were humbled, they developed a woe-is-me attitude. Some of them may have lumbered around in sackcloth, if they had any.

But humility is not about putting ourselves down. Humility involves recognizing our need for forgiveness and God's graciousness in offering it to us. And that's reason to celebrate! So then the Israelites ate, they drank, and they shared their possessions so no one was excluded. They were humbled and grateful, thus honoring the Lord in their party.

Consider the instructions Nehemiah and Ezra issued to be joyful, and look at how children and dogs romp, fully delighting in God's creation in their play. God wants you to experience His goodness now, not just later! And since there's no time like the present. . . .

Lord, thank You for Your grace, and all the ways I experience Your goodness. I rejoice today!

RUNNING ON SAND

*Everyone who competes in the games goes into strict training. They do it to get
a crown that will not last; but we do it to get a crown that will last forever.*

1 CORINTHIANS 9:25 NIV

Ask any runner–the beach offers challenging terrain. Some run barefoot while others wear shoes, but those who appear to stride effortlessly have been at it a while. They have had to train and build up strength to make it look so easy.

Running on a softer surface requires better balance and more energy from the muscles involved. There are plenty of risks too, such as sprains, strains, and puncture wounds. So why do it?

The payoff is worth it! These runners improve their strength, they experience less impact on their joints, and they burn more calories per mile. Training on a beach can literally put more spring in their step when they run on a hard surface like asphalt.

At times, running the race God sets for each of us seems more difficult than living a mediocre, milquetoast life. But if the races of faith were easy, everyone would be running them.

As Paul explained, our race centers around one goal–a life that's pleasing to God, achieved by "strict training"–and one prize–"A crown that will last forever." Challenging terrain aside, aren't God's pleasure and an everlasting reward worth everything?

*Father God, help me to persevere when I'm weary
and to keep my eyes on the end result.*

THE BEAUTY REMAINS

O God, You have taught me from my youth; and to
this day I declare Your wondrous works.

PSALM 71:17 NKJV

T ake a look around the beach. You may see distressed wood, oxidized iron, and boats and dock posts bearing barnacles. In another time, these objects were new, pristine, pretty. But now they are chipped, dented, tired, careworn. They're no longer new, but their beauty remains: they wear the look of time, experience, hardships, and authenticity.

Maybe you're in a season where, like the distressed items, you feel past your prime. Perhaps you were pretty, you had a great career, or you thrived on motherhood. You had a certain positive identity, but it no longer exists (sometimes by choice). Most days you are at peace, but some days the what-ifs and what-might-have-beens creep in and guilt follows.

Remember that distressed items reflect wear because they were well used. Many a beach house or boat is furnished and decorated with distressed items; their display reminds us that what they did mattered for the long haul. Their contribution carried part of our world's story to the next step. The same holds true with people.

No matter the changes that have altered your identity, you are by no means finished. Even though the sun has set on a particular point in your life, your work is not done. You see, your marks of distress are actually marks of distinction. Your life choices, your hurts, your victories all are there on display. Your contribution carried our collective story to the next step. Your next contribution will too; you will continue to "declare [His] wondrous works."

Lord, let my life stories serve as a testimony to Your glory—
and together, let's move on to the next adventure.

BEACH BOULDERS

"Whoever hears these sayings of Mine, and does them, I will
liken him to a wise man who built his house on the rock."

MATTHEW 7:24 NKJV

If you've climbed on any beach boulders, you've probably slipped a time or two. But once you reached the top, once you were secure on that solid structure and looked out safely at the waves below, there was something truly remarkable in knowing that they could splash you, but they could not carry you away.

There's a reason boulders are immune to storms: these large, sturdy rocks are so heavy they are immovable. Some have been around for thousands of years, unmoved by time or conditions.

In today's Scripture, Jesus was talking about how to live intelligently: obey His teachings, thereby building a secure foundation that is safe against storms. Troubles and pain have the same effects on our hearts that waves do when we're seated on a boulder: they lap over us. At times these waves may appear stronger than our rock, but as soon as they break against our foundation, they shatter and disperse.

We cannot avoid strife and difficulties this side of heaven. But thanks to Jesus, when the waves are high we can pray, "Reach down from heaven and rescue me; rescue me from deep waters" (Psalm 144:7), and our foundation will hold. He will break those hard times and give us the power to manage and endure, just like a beach boulder.

Lord, thank You for Your teachings, which serve
as my foundation and a safe place to rest.

SALT-AIR HAIR

There is no wisdom, no insight, no plan that can succeed against the LORD.

PROVERBS 21:30 NIV

When we visit the beach, why does our hair frizz, turn into unwanted curls or a lack of them, or flail out in flyaways? Our hair just frustrates us as it blows around in the salty breeze.

We smooth it down. We may even comb conditioner through it. Or we stuff it into a loose bun or ponytail, hoping that will keep wild strands in check. We might as well give up! We have salt-air hair.

Today's verse wasn't written with salt-air hair in mind, but beach-blown hair can remind us of this truth: some things are just out of our control. And our best efforts, no matter how intelligent or skillful they are, cannot succeed against God.

We can laugh about this when it comes to frizzy beach hair; we can even try to embrace our over-curly locks. But there are times when the situation is not so funny, times when evil seems to be winning: our child is being bullied, our best friend is making a destructive decision, or a boss's words are cutting and dismissive.

No matter how things appear, God instructs us to let Him guide us in all things (Proverbs 3:5–6). We know that His answers alone will succeed–"The victory belongs to the LORD" (Proverbs 21:31). Savor this truth and leave the hair gel behind today! Let your hair fly free as a reminder that your soul does as well.

Father God, I don't have to worry about how to
fix all the problems in life; You will take care of
them. That frees me, and I thank You!

SOMETHING'S MISSING

[I] have poured out my soul before the LORD.

1 SAMUEL 1:15 NKJV

A boat without a sail. A net without a fish. A crab shell without a crab in it. Some things just don't look right when something's missing. It's the same for us as human beings: when we lack something that feels essential, we feel out of sorts, even desperate.

The biblical character Hannah longed for a child. No one could comfort her. Her well-intended husband discounted her feelings and questioned why he wasn't family enough for her (1 Samuel 1:8). Hannah did what we all can do when we urgently need something: she invited the Lord's intervention.

Isn't it tough to live in a state of longing? Perhaps in your time of need, friends or family have lectured you about focusing on your blessings or questioned the depth of your faith. Although they mean well, loved ones may reinforce feelings that something is wrong with us because we feel so strongly about the situation, event, or result we long for. But those criticisms don't change the desire.

As long as you feel like a boat without a sail, keep seeking that missing part. Pray like Hannah, and when the Lord answers, rejoice like Hannah too (1 Samuel 2:1–10).

Lord, give me peace and patience as I wait on You, and show me how my longing may be used to Your glory.

A SOUL AT REST

Return to your rest, O my soul, for the LORD has dealt bountifully with you.

PSALM 116:7 NKJV

What's your favorite way to relax at the beach? Nap in a hammock? Soak up rays? Enjoy the early morning breeze on a screened-in porch? Fish off the dock? Close your eyes and let the sound of the waves lull you to sleep?

We are, by design, required to rest. Even Jesus needed sleep and downtime. It's an opportunity for our minds and bodies to replenish and renew. Rest balances out our work and the stresses of everyday life.

But what does it mean for our souls to be at rest? What is the peace Jesus referred to when He greeted His disciples after His resurrection: "Peace be with you" (Luke 24:36)? Is it possible for our bodies and minds to be in motion and our souls to remain at rest? If so, how?

The author of Psalm 116 had not just been discouraged; he'd experienced great suffering. He called, he begged, he implored the Lord to help him. He was nearly overcome by "trouble and sorrow" and felt "the pains of death" (v. 3 NKJV). But he maintained enough faith to seek the Lord's deliverance; he didn't give up. The result: "I was brought low, [but] He saved me" (v. 6 NKJV).

As you rock in your hammock or have a quiet morning moment with coffee and your Bible, think about the times God has delivered you. Consider the blessings He has showered upon you. When troubles come, remember His faithfulness, and find rest for your soul.

Father, I am so grateful for the many times You have delivered me. Whether in quiet or calamity, my soul will be at rest because You are there.

A SOUL-HEALING SUNRISE

*Let the morning bring me word of your unfailing love, for I have put my
trust in you. Show me the way I should go, for to you I entrust my life.*

PSALM 143:8 NIV

Tonight even the soft sounds of the waves do not soothe. You're restless. Maybe you're anxious about tomorrow. Or perhaps something else is gnawing at you, an issue from your past or a dilemma in the present. Regardless, you're distracted. You need daylight to break through.

Sunrises hold so much promise: a new day, a new opportunity, a fresh start. If you've lost the opportunity for sleep, get up and watch the sun spill over the horizon. Witnessing a sunrise at the beach is a soul-healing process. As the intense colors emerge and break across the ocean, consider what our Lord said about worry: we are not to fret about tomorrow, for "each day has enough trouble of its own" (Matthew 6:34 NIV). Whatever troubles are stealing your sleep, it's time to hand them over to the One who can wrangle them.

It's clear from Psalm 143 that David prayed in the nighttime; he too must have lost sleep. His prayer is a good one for us to emulate: he asked for the light of the Lord to shine along with the light from the sun. He reminded God that he trusted Him. Don't all of us need to say such things?

When even calm waves don't soothe, remember that dawn is coming. A fresh start. A new day. A clean slate. Watch for the Lord as you watch for the sun.

*Lord, thank You for the sunrise. It reminds me
that as each day starts anew, so can I.*

DON'T WILT

"With God everything is possible."

MATTHEW 19:26

Pick up a handful of dry sand. Think about the tiny grains that together make up the entire beach. A small handful is easily moved, but moving an entire beach would be impossible.

Consider the burdens the Israelites bore as recorded in Nehemiah: forced to live in a foreign country, they learned their beloved Jerusalem's wall lay in shambles. Then God raised a leader to restore the wall. Nehemiah miraculously obtained permission to depart Babylon to rebuild; then he organized the Israelites and began restoration. But confronted with ridicule and threats, the Israelites wilted.

How many times have we started a project without completing it? Nehemiah took seriously his responsibility. He confronted those who tried to sabotage the work. Nehemiah knew that failure would be disobedience to God. The result? The Israelites completed the city's wall in just fifty-two days. What an accomplishment!

Look again at a handful of sand. Watch how individually the grains blow in the wind, but when packed together they form a beach that may shift and change, yet always remains intact.

Have you written off a task as impossible? If God provides, are you willing to be responsible with what He's given you to do? Don't wilt–stand strong under pressure! "With God everything is possible"!

Lord, when I'm tasked with a seemingly impossible project,
give me a determined heart so I won't get discouraged.

A SIP OF SALT WATER

You can't draw fresh water from a salty spring.

JAMES 3:12

D o you remember the first time you sampled ocean water? Was the taste a shock to your system? Did you find yourself breathlessly running to find clear water to rinse with?

Our own anger, when it flares unexpectedly, can be a shock to the system too. We gasp, so inflamed with hurt or pride that the breath won't come. Just like the first time we discovered the ocean's salty water, we're startled in a way that leaves us reeling.

Does your speech or behavior affect others this way? Do you consider how you deliver your ideas or opinions? Are your words and actions "gracious and attractive" (Colossians 4:6), or are they traumatizing?

The tongue is a tricky mechanism. James described it as "a tiny spark" that "can set a great forest on fire" (James 3:5). It can build up or level a person more swiftly than anything.

When you're angry, whittle down to the real reason for it. If discipline or confrontation must ensue, remember, the goal is to reconcile, not retaliate. Ask God to provide the right words and attitude. Plan to respond with great care, keeping peaceful resolve your goal.

Just as a sip of salt water can shock your body into breathlessness and immediate thirst, so angry words and acts can stun a loved one into pain and confusion. Let caution carve out a better release for your emotions.

Lord, as I splash about in the salty ocean today, remind me of the effects of my speech and behavior. I want to love others well.

WIPEOUT

He reached down from on high and took hold of me; he drew me out of deep waters.

PSALM 18:16 NIV

Relaxed in your beach chair, minding your own business, you've hit that lull between awake and sleep. You still hear the sounds around you, but they seem soft and distant.

Wham! A wave crashes right over your knees, whisking away your magazine, sunglasses, water bottle, and flip-flops. You recall that the tide was out when you first sat down, but more time must have passed than you thought. You scramble to pick up what you can and *wham!* Another wave hits! Your arms full of relaxation accoutrements, you hurriedly head for higher ground.

We can be overtaken in life too. Waves of all kinds can wipe out our peace of mind, a special relationship, a savings account, a prized position. Regardless of what caused the wave, something valuable has been lost, and we're struggling to find our footing.

You might think you exist in a place of despair. You can't imagine recovering from your particular wave; in fact, you're afraid you'll drown. But look at King David's testimony in Psalm 18: God "reached down," "took hold," "drew [him] out of deep waters." You are not–you are never–beyond God's reach.

The tide will recede again. You'll find yourself on dry land. You will regain your footing. Don't let the reality of wipeouts blur the edges of your faith in God's goodness. Sudden waves happen, but God is always ready to rescue you.

Lord, lift me up; show me how to stand again on solid ground.

A BEACH ROMANCE

You shall love the LORD your God with all your heart,
with all your soul, and with all your strength.

DEUTERONOMY 6:5 NKJV

The beach just lends itself to romance–to long walks with a loved one along the surf with hands entwined, casual dinners overlooking the bay, relaxing on the sand, cuddling in a cabana. It can be the perfect setting for couples to relax and just enjoy each other's company, whether they are reigniting their love or discovering it for the first time.

The beach is also a perfect setting to reignite our love for God.

We know we love the Lord. We know He loves us. But how often do we say it with full and grateful hearts? As we're absorbing the glory of His creation oceanside, do we recall that we are in the Creator's presence, remember that His love provided this view, this trip, or this loved one?

God pursues us. He listens. He reassures us. He keeps His promises. He provides. He gives good gifts. If any human being does this much for us, we most certainly let that person know our appreciation. So why not thank the One who breathed our lovely beach surroundings into existence? Is it possible that actually saying it may be a way to love Him with "all [our] strength"?

At the beach, love your love–and remember to love the Lord of love, out loud.

Lord, I am so thankful for Your many, many blessings,
including the gift of this oceanside retreat. I love You.

BROKEN IS BEAUTIFUL

*"You shall open your hand wide to your brother, to
your poor and your needy, in your land."*

DEUTERONOMY 15:11 NKJV

S eashells come in all shapes and sizes. The selections and quantities differ at high and low tides, after storms, and in various locations. Our collections may last a day, or a lifetime. But what about the broken shells? Do we ever stop for those?

We can ask the same about the people we encounter. As with seashells, we certainly have our favorites–the ones we seek out, ones we notice. Others we discover by accident or circumstance, and we're grateful to gather them too. Some encounters result in lifelong relationships, while others may last only a few minutes. But what about the broken people? Do we see them?

Sometimes they are clearly shattered, and we look away. On others the fractures are barely visible until we're very close to them. Whether the wounds are obvious or not, often we're hesitant to respond in a personal way. We don't want drama. We don't want to risk exposure to someone's hardship, lest it burden us. We have enough trouble keeping our lives stable, let alone the life of someone without resources.

But God says, "You shall open your hand wide to your brother." When we care for the broken, we care for the Lord Himself–He said so (Matthew 25:40).

Pick up a shell fragment and carry it as a reminder that, just like seashells, some people are whole. Some are broken. All are beautiful and valuable to God.

*Dear Lord, make me aware of those who need help,
and help me offer it quickly and generously.*

UMBRELLA TRIBE

*Whoever dwells in the shelter of the Most High will
rest in the shadow of the Almighty.*

PSALM 91:1 NIV

B each umbrellas' polka dots, rainbow colors, floral designs, and plaid patterns decorate the sand with their colorful canopies. These umbrellas are staked in the sand like flags marking the home base of each beach tribe, made up of families, friends, or both.

If you belong to the tribe, you enjoy the freedom of coming and going to the umbrella location, which acts like a storing station for bags, food items, coolers, sunscreen, and every beach necessity under the sun. It's the place children know to return to find their families after wading in the ocean or building a sand castle. Groups of friends throwing a football or batting a volleyball run back to the umbrella's shelter to cool down and regroup. Friend and family crews know to return to their umbrella for whatever they need.

If God had an umbrella on the beach, it would be the main attraction. His food stock would be unbeatable–sweet watermelon and grapes, crackers and cheese, choice meats and cooling beverages. And His toys would be the best–elaborate sand castle molds, giant dolphin-shaped inflatable rafts, and every sport ball imaginable. We would all be welcome because He provides more than enough room for us in His shade. Here under God's great wing, like an umbrella spread out on the beach just for His tribe, we find our home base for life.

*Father, remind me to rest and recharge under
the shadow of Your "umbrella."*

A PATIENT PACE

*Your life is now hidden with Christ in God. When Christ, who is
your life, appears, then you also will appear with him in glory.*

COLOSSIANS 3:3–4 NIV

O ff the shores of tropical beaches, coral reefs are sturdy and anchored. They form when a polyp, a soft-bodied animal, attaches to the sea floor and multiplies into a colony. These coral families supply limestone to build a hard, protective foundation that grows less than an inch each year. Yet, unlike stone, these oceanic boulders are alive. Coral life–some thorny, some spongy, some treelike–form underwater ecosystems of astonishing beauty and diversity.

Coral reefs provide homes for thousands of sea creatures in their spikes, nooks, polyp forests, and open, stony meadows. The greatest variety of sea life exists in the coral reefs: they are the jungles of the ocean, vibrant and bursting with communities of fish, sea turtles, crustaceans, and microscopic life, even as they appear still and merely decorative.

The pace of the coral reef's growth–thousands of years–is a picture of patience. It's a picture we should apply to our own growth as we become the people God made us to be. The fact is, it takes *time* to achieve the deep and steady maturation that ignites our faith and grows our gifts. If we surrender to God's pace and let Him shape us, we flourish with life–life we can share with others as a source of abundance and support.

*Jesus, before I hurry to good works, hide my life in Yours
and carry me along in patience and steady growth.*

SAILING AMONG THE CLOUDS

Since we are surrounded by so great a cloud of
witnesses, let us also lay aside every weight.

Hebrews 12:1 esv

The boat takes off, cutting through the ocean waves, and you are lifted up, the canopy of the parasail catching the rushing wind. You soar high into the sky. Parasailing is a weightless, exhilarating ride across the coast.

Unlike hang-glider pilots or skydivers, the parasailer has no control over direction or anything else: he or she is locked in and strapped to the boat's every move. In the same way, our salvation is completely accomplished through the works of Jesus. When we believe in Him, it's as if He attaches a parasailing rope to Himself and a sail to us. Our part is to let go of what weighs us down, what ties us tightly to earth, and let the "boat" of Christ lead us to heaven.

When worldliness tries to weigh you down, hold on to the straps of the sail that carries you upward. Look at the clouds around you in the air, which are like the saints of God in heaven, "a great cloud of witnesses" cheering you on toward eternity. Drop whatever you carry that's heavy, and let yourself be borne up to experience the exhilaration of a sky-high ride to your free salvation; it's a joyous trip without the weight of the world.

Father, keep me tethered to Jesus, and show me what
I can let go of to sail more freely toward home.

A SEAHORSE'S TAIL

I press on toward the goal for the prize of the upward call of God in Christ Jesus.

PHILIPPIANS 3:14 ESV

O ut of all the creatures of the ocean, the seahorse is the most curiously cute. It has a head like a horse's with a trumpet-like snout that looks as if it might announce its procession through the waters. Beady eyes and erect ears give it an expression of constant surprise. Its body may be spiny or spotted or neon colored. The seahorse is a fascinating creature, straight out of the imagination of our Creator and Father.

In His wisdom, God did not doom the little horse-fish to stay suspended in the water. He fashioned a dorsal fin and delicate pectoral fins that flutter rapidly to usher it forward. To move up and down, the seahorse adjusts the volume of an air-filled sac. It also harnesses its most unique attribute–its curling tail. Seahorses grasp plants on the sea floor and coral to hold themselves in place. They use all of the parts of their godly design for locomotion. They were made to move forward, and so are we.

The most precious, curious gifts God gives us can be our greatest assets to help push us toward our "upward call of God in Christ Jesus." The unique talents we hide because the world might disqualify them as odd or insignificant, like a seahorse's tail, God stamps with the affirmation of heaven. If we harness every part of ourselves into moving onward with God, we will gain ground and He will be glorified.

God, point out the rare gifts You've placed in me and bring them to life as I move forward confidently with You.

THE PLEASURE OF HIS PRESENCE

His anointing teaches you about everything . . . just
as it has taught you, abide in him.

1 JOHN 2:27 ESV

How would you picture the anointing of God's Holy Spirit? Like a thunderstorm, powerfully drenching you in thick, pounding drops of rain? Or like soaking in sunrays or feeling a cooling ocean wave washing over your feet? In whatever form His Spirit comes, we do experience powerful moments of anointing that direct our purpose toward the kingdom. But what about the ordinary days of simple, loyal living for the Lord?

Most of us will spend most of our days in the ordinary, everyday abiding in the sweetness of the Lord's presence. We do not have to venture off on a missionary call, start a new philanthropic business endeavor, or generate a political campaign for Him in order to receive His anointing and His aid.

We also don't have to wait for dramatic moments to know He is with us. Instead, when we hear the gospel and believe in Him, we are sealed with the anointing of the Holy Spirit for life (Ephesians 4:13). His presence never abandons us, even during seemingly mundane moments.

Exciting times will come when we do great deeds for Him, and then His anointing may feel like a powerful beach rainstorm. But in the everyday, simple abiding, the anointing of God's Spirit is more like the warmth of the beach sun beaming all around us. Enjoy the pleasure of His presence and the anointing of His Spirit.

God, teach me to dwell in Your presence
in my everyday moments.

ARMOR UP!

Put on the whole armor of God, that you may be able
to stand against the schemes of the devil.

EPHESIANS 6:11 ESV

S cuba diving is a popular beach excursion, and every diver wears the appro-
priate equipment in order to survive while exploring underwater worlds.
The mask protects your eyes and clarifies your view. The scuba regulator trans-
fers air from the scuba tank to your mouth. The fins or flippers help you swim
and navigate efficiently, and the wet suit warms and protects your skin. Each
piece of equipment helps ensure a successful visit to under-the-sea wonders.

Similarly, each part of the armor Paul described in Ephesians 6:14–17 is necessary to help us successfully complete God's mission in our lives. God has made
us the ambassadors of His redemption story–a bold move, as we are often weak
on our own. Our personal inadequacy alerts us to armor up, so we put on the
belt of truth, the breastplate of righteousness, the shield of faith, and the helmet
of salvation. This precious covering, these spiritual tools, aid us in deflecting the
darts of the enemy so we can bring forth God's plans and kingdom.

This armor doesn't weigh us down; it enables us to thrive in our mission to
minister the kingdom of light. Like scuba divers jumping into watery depths,
we use the proper gear so we can thwart evil "schemes" and reveal God's plan
of redemption. Just as you would never travel underwater without scuba equipment, don't take the gospel into the world without the armor of God.

Father, give me the tools I need to be an effective part of Your
good plan for creation, prepared to outplay the evil one.

MANTA RAY MAGIC

Jesus Christ is the same yesterday and today and forever.

HEBREWS 13:8 ESV

Manta rays glide through shallow waters by the shore, arcing gradually up and then sliding back down, riding underwater waves. Although they resemble stingrays, they don't have the sting. They are harmless plankton eaters with diamond-shaped, flat, supple bodies, with a tail tagging behind. If you peer intently into the shallow coastal waters, they are viewable from the beach, and a delight to watch traveling in a row along the coast.

At least the adults are. Juveniles, on the other hand, have eluded marine biologists for decades—until recently. Scientists discovered the first manta ray nursery hidden at the bottom of the sea in a marine sanctuary. They were there all along—where scientists have been studying sea animals and their homes since it was founded. They could have looked all over the unexplored wide ocean, but the manta ray juveniles were where they had been researching for years.

Sometimes we lose sight of the Lord, particularly when life seems as vast and uncharted as the ocean. When change comes or we are confused by the direction life has taken, we may be disoriented and wonder where God is in our expanding world. But He was there all along. Often He is where we originally found Him—in church, in the Bible, with trusted friends and family, and in nature. He hasn't moved on us. Seek Him wholeheartedly and in sincerity for who He truly is, and He will be found. Unlike the manta ray babies, He is right where you'd expect Him to be—on the throne and in control.

Jesus, when I'm disoriented by changing circumstances,
strengthen my connection to our steadfast, constant Father.

JELLYFISH GLOWING IN THE DARK

The Lord my God lightens my darkness.

PSALM 18:28 ESV

If you are fortunate enough to witness a jellyfish float to the top of the water while safely on a boat, or observe them in a colony from behind an aquarium tank wall, our buoyant, ocean-dwelling friends are fascinating to behold.

Jellyfish are striking creatures without ears, hearts, or brains. They can be as small as a thumbnail (Irukandji jellyfish) or as long as 120 feet (the lion's mane jellyfish) or as heavy as 440 pounds (Nomura's jellyfish). They come in different colors, but all share the trait of translucency. They flap melodically, pulsing through the water as if swimming to a classical symphony. And their most captivating trick: some jellyfish glow in the dark.

Nothing draws our attention like a bright light in utter darkness. Our eyes follow jellyfish lit up with bioluminescent organs as they flit about deep blue water. In a world that can seem as dark as the black vacuum of the ocean's depths, God is our light. There is no darkness in Him at all (1 John 1:5).

Jellyfish are often unwelcome finds in the deepest, darkest places, but there is no need to fear those places when you know the Lord. His light penetrates and reveals. His good purpose is to make us as beautiful and mesmerizing as a jellyfish so others will be drawn to His light in us.

God, let Your light shine through me to brighten a dim world in need of You.

THE TEETER-TOTTER BIRDS

There is nothing better for a person than that he should eat and drink and
find enjoyment in his toil. This also . . . is from the hand of God.

ECCLESIASTES 2:24 ESV

Sandpipers are observed by beach dwellers every year as their eating habits cause a rhythmic scurrying down the shoreline. They follow the fluctuating tide with quick, tiny movements of their sticklike legs. They race with the the water, picking out insects, crustaceans, and worms from the wet sand. They have thin, long beaks and rounded bodies that end in a point.

There is one type, however, that exhibits an unusual trait unlike any other shorebird: the spotted sandpiper. These guys bob their tails up and down, causing their rounded, white, spotted bodies to wobble back and forth continually. They teeter! And it's awfully cute. Scientists don't know why they do it, but as soon as they are freshly hatched, the little chicks immediately start teetering as if born to do it just for fun. This performance makes the little shorebirds appear giddy about the common tasks of catching food and roaming their sandy homes.

We can find a similar bounce in our steps when we are assured of our home in heaven and that our lives please God. If you let yourself enjoy the simplicity of daily tasks, you might catch yourself humming, singing, maybe even bobbing a little like a spotted sandpiper.

Father, show me how to enjoy the simplicity of
daily tasks, enough to put a pep in my step.

CONCH SHELLS HOLD THE OCEAN

"The words that I have spoken to you are spirit and life."

JOHN 6:63 ESV

O n an early beach morning, you are still drowsy, and your resting frame matches the stillness of the ground and celestial sphere. But watching the contrasting vibrancy of the ocean against the serenity of the beach wakes you up on the inside. It sets your feet walking along the shore. As you follow a mosaic-tiled trail of cracked shells engrained lightly in the sand, a startling sight stops you in your tracks. You've spotted a treasure washed up onshore and lying in the damp sand to the right–a queen conch shell.

The shell is fully intact. Spines rim the spiral up to the point. The tan and cream curvature of the shell meets the orange pink of the lip at the opening, and the inside holds the ocean. Lift it up and cup it to your ear, and you'll see what I mean. The shell's cavity reverberates with ambient sounds that reach your ear and seem to carry the whooshing of waves and winds.

Just as the sea delivered the shell to the shore, God has given us His words that are spirit and life, recorded for us in the Bible. When you need to be awakened to all God has in store for your day, when the world seems still and void of life, pick up your Bible. You will read His direct words and come alive inside so that every day and every season, you are as awake as the ocean.

*God, help me have the discipline to read Your
Word so that my spirit is stirred to life.*

HEARTS FRESH OUT OF THE SHELL

May the Lord direct your hearts into God's love and Christ's perseverance.

2 THESSALONIANS 3:5 NIV

When sea turtles hatch out of their eggs, they are vulnerable to seagull, raccoon, and ghost crab. With their paddlelike legs, tiny, delicate shells, and fresh, newborn eyes, these brand-new creatures must find their way from the beach nesting spot to the ocean waters.

When we become, by divine mercy, born-again believers, our hearts are fresh out of their shells of fear and worldly trappings and ushered toward true life and godly adventure. We may suddenly recognize that our new hearts of tender flesh are vulnerable to schemes, tricks, snares, or sins.

But as with God's baby sea turtles, He does not leave us without direction. The sea turtles may use the slope of the shore, the white splashes of waves breaking, the light of the horizon, and even the magnetic field of the earth. Once they reach the ocean, the young turtles will find currents to usher them toward their sea homes.

In the same way, the Lord directs our hearts toward His love and perseverance with guidance of Scripture, the light of His presence, and words of encouragement. At first you might feel as awkward as a young sea turtle trying to use flippers to walk. But keep your eyes on the cues of heaven to guide you to the ocean of God's protective love, where His currents will push you forward to your next destination.

*Father, lead me to the currents of Your love
for ongoing energy and strength.*

THE PARROT-FISH SPECIALTY

"Put out into the deep and let down your nets for a catch."

Luke 5:4 esv

P arrot fish have scales that match the colorful plumage of the exotic bird they are named after, and protruding mouths shaped almost like beaks. These herbivores have specialized, constantly growing teeth to reach the algae in coral reefs.

Jesus' first followers were fishermen, and like parrot fish, they specialized in capturing their food a certain way. They were raised to catch fish and knew the tricks of the trade. When the men had been fishing one night with no luck, Simon Peter obeyed the suggestion of a stranger to let down the nets again.

You can imagine, at the first tug of the net, Peter's eyes widening as he grabbed with both hands and heaved up a net bursting with fish. This miraculous haul shocked and rocked him. But Jesus met Peter's panic with a calm command: *Don't be afraid. You will be catching people from now on.* To common fisherman Peter, this must have sounded as odd as a fish being named after a bird!

As we become fishers of people, we might feel inadequate; people might not respond. Jesus reassures us, "Don't be afraid" (Luke 5:10 niv). We may think we are qualified only for our particular line of work, like algae-eating parrot fish. But He has equipped us for capturing the hearts of men and women for Him, no matter our area of worldly expertise.

*Jesus, You are welcome in any boat of my
life. Help me win souls to Your love.*

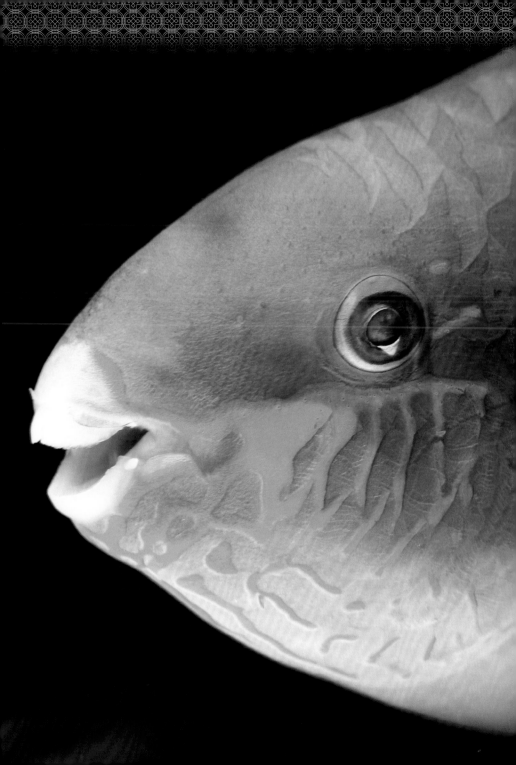

CHAIRS IN THE TIDE

All have sinned and fall short of the glory of God,
and are justified by his grace as a gift.

ROMANS 3:23–24 ESV

Have you ever placed your chair on the beach right on the ocean's rim? It may be the most relaxing spot on shore. The chair legs sink into the wet sand so that you are completely stationary. Leaning back and lying still, feeling the breeze, you unwind as the waves come up and cool your feet as the tide tickles your toes. This is what vacations are made of.

When we receive the grace of God, it's like taking a vacation for our soul. In a world where we are conditioned, educated, and trained on how to work for a living for food, entertainment, and daily needs, it's easy to translate this work mentality to church and faith. Surely we must work as hard, if not harder, to be good and righteous enough for God, to get to partake in His gifts, peace, and promises. No wonder, when we fail in these attempts, that we feel defeated, maybe even angry or depressed: we didn't hit the mark.

The Bible assures us that no one has hit the mark, but goodness and righteousness have already been attained for us. We are justified, made right, brought up to heavenly standards as a gift freely given by Jesus. Our souls can sit in beach chairs by the tide, lean back, and soak up the warmth of God's radiant love. The ocean waves wash our feet just as Jesus washes us.

Jesus, my soul needs a vacation from striving toward
unrealistic standards. Sit me by Your cleansing
waters and help me receive Your goodness freely.

PORCH PERSPECTIVES

God, being rich in mercy . . . raised us up with [Jesus]
and seated us with him in the heavenly places.

EPHESIANS 2:4, 6 ESV

P orch views from the higher levels of beach houses or condos that overlook the ocean offer an earthly version of a heavenly view. Standing by
the railing, surveying the beach environment below, you can see it all: sand
dunes with grasses growing over low, rolling hills, with paths in between that
lead to the wide-open stretches to the right and left. The sand-carpet coast
meets the ocean tide, rhythmically flowing in and rolling back out in shallow
waves. The waters farther out in the open ocean are calm and stretch all the way
to the silent, steady horizon. The entire artistic vista is one painted by God.

Sometimes when we are stuck down in the drama of life, it's natural to lose
the eternal view, to stop seeing how the trivial matters of our days can add up
to lives filled with purpose. But when we engage with God, when we pray, read
Scripture, and talk about matters of eternal importance with friends and family, God reminds us He has seated us with Christ in heavenly places. Our vision
for life is renewed, and once again we see from a higher vantage point where we
can get a glimpse of it all–the beautiful portrait painted by God.

God, when life seems messy and incongruent,
bring me up to Your heavenly view to see the
picture You are painting with my life.

SAND DOLLAR BANK

"Come, everyone who thirsts, come to the waters; and
he who has no money, come, buy and eat!"

ISAIAH 55:1 ESV

S and dollars are the mystical money of beach shores. They look like big, white, chalky coins with their star or flower designs pressed on the top center of each circle. When sand dollars are alive, they are actually purple, green, or blue sea urchins. In the ocean, sand dollars are active in colonies. They are like a living currency.

It takes imagination and a childlike heart to picture a sand dollar as make-believe money. Pretend money delights children, and Jesus says we must become like them to enter the kingdom (Mark 10:15). God tells us to come to buy, eat, and drink from His heavenly storehouse without money; when it comes to the kingdom, we are better off with a bank full of sand dollars. We come to God for what real-world money cannot purchase: value as individuals, affirmation of our identities, inspiration for our dreams, and faith to carry us forward.

When we need words of love and assurance that we are wealthy and not bankrupt in the deep ways that matter, we can go to God, who gives to us freely. He'll give us true drink and true food that nourish our souls without cost. But handing Him some sand dollars in return sure would make Him smile.

Father, fill my bank with the treasures of heaven, not
the worldly materials that never fully satisfy.

POOLSIDE RETREAT

How lovely is your dwelling place, O LORD of hosts! My
soul longs, yes, faints for the courts of the LORD.

PSALM 84:1–2 ESV

The sun beams down on your face, and droplets of perspiration roll down your cheeks. You are smiling and exuberant from a day on the beach, but also exhausted and sticky from the salty blend of sweat and seawater. By this point, the heat is clinging and relentless. You're downright faint.

You enjoy the hearty, worn-out feeling from beach play, but it's time for a break, and the pool area by the condominium is calling. The crystal-blue, chlorinated-clean water as cool as the spot right in front of a fan seems sublime. Trading the sand floors for the concrete of the pool area will be a respite.

When we are out working for God in our jobs, ministries, and homes, like fatigued beach revelers we need a recess. Family life is busy and filled with chores to get done; at work and in ministry we connect with people, sometimes butt heads, and learn how to live together in community. We can get rumpled and tired from our interactions and tasks, but it is good. It is a worthy way to extend our energies, yet we also need a break. When the courts of God are calling like a pool retreat, go to that place, wherever it is for you.

Find a sanctuary, and let the purifying waters of God wash, cool, and cleanse you. This retreat will refresh your mind, and you'll remember that your day-to-day efforts, are all worth giving and worthy of God's attention. Once refreshed, get back out there. The pool area is pleasant, but the beach is bursting with glorious action.

God, You are my enduring place of retreat. Replenish me in Your sanctuary, where I find steady care and fresh energy.

CAPTURING CRUSTACEANS

Your word is a lamp to my feet and a light to my path.

PSALM 119:105 NKJV

Crab hunting is an extreme sport for some beach-going families. Once a crab hunt has been declared, excitement builds and preparation begins—people gladly gather nets, sandals, shovels, buckets for the ambitious, and most important, flashlights. As soon as the sun dips behind the ocean's end, and the moon flips its light switch on, the creepy, crawling crabs come out of their holes, twinkling about with starlight on their backs.

Oh, the thrill of seeing an eight-legged crustacean scurry right across the spotlight made by your flashlight. Giggles and a chase follow, then shouts of joy for your friends and family to join your discovery. Capturing the crabs and placing them in the buckets or nets means victory. But could you imagine hunting crabs without a flashlight? Not only would you miss what you are searching for, you couldn't see where you were going and—what was that crunch under your feet? No thank you!

What in life do you want to catch? True friendships, a wholesome lifestyle, ministry opportunities? And what do you need to avoid that would hinder your progress forward? Trying to seek good things and avoid bad ones without the light from God's Word is like trying to capture crabs without a flashlight. God's Word is the lamp to illuminate and clarify your way. It will make your steps confident so you can shout for joy when you find victory, calling your friends over to celebrate God's goodness with you.

Jesus, lead me to Scriptures that will brighten my path
and guide me to victorious moments for Your glory.

HUNGRY HERONS

"Ask, and it will be given to you; seek, and you will
find; knock, and it will be opened to you."

MATTHEW 7:7 ESV

A little way from the ocean, across a street and behind beach homes, you can sometimes find marine wetlands that hold docks and boats like miniature marinas. They're hidden from the busier beach areas, quieter, and still. These places can be wildlife havens where creatures will come out and exhibit brazen behaviors in a place that's proven familiar and safe.

If you sit on one of these docks at dusk, don't be surprised if a great blue heron feels comfortable to sit near you. And don't be alarmed when he seems to stare at you unabashedly. The seabird is probably used to having the boat owners and fishers sneak him a fishy snack from their hauls every now and then. These herons' impudent gazes courageously ask for a share of the day's take.

Because of the bird's bold stare, a kindly fisherman will sometimes relent and toss a snack. You can learn from this creature's bold look. When we want or need something from our heavenly Father, He desires that we ask, seek, and knock. We do that foremost in prayer, but also in circumstances and opportunities where He leads us. Seek what you want, ask around for connections to what you need, and even bravely knock on those doors in your life. Like a heron in a hidden marina, you'll find a seat next to the Lord is a familiar and safe place in which to make requests with confidence.

Father, teach me how to ask You for what I need, in the
resolute faith that comes from knowing I'm Your child.

UNDERWATER WORLD

"My kingdom is not of this world."

John 18:36 NKJV

The underwater ocean world is like a hidden kingdom away from ordinary life on land. On the earth we are in an atmosphere of air, much dryer than the watery substance of the sea. We have brick buildings and paved roads. The sea's buildings are natural mounds of calcium carbonate reefs, and the highways are water currents. The trees on land sway in the breeze; the seaweed of the ocean melodically moves in liquid slow motion.

Perhaps the greatest difference, obvious but invisible, is the way creatures breathe. As we know, in the ocean oxygen is sipped from the water and on land, the air. The world, the one Jesus refers to, runs on a different source of oxygen from the one His followers rely on. The two groups, and methods of breathing, are as different as the sea and the land.

The world runs on or uses material possessions, career success, opinions of people, riches, vain beauty, and fame as oxygen, or a means of feeling alive. People consume and seem never to have enough. The kingdom of heaven operates as opposite to this as if it were underwater. The "oxygen" of the kingdom is joy, peace, and selfless love and service. This kind of oxygen satisfies.

The best choice for an intake that gives the breath of life is the kingdom of Jesus, set apart from the world like an underwater palace that never runs out of revitalizing, heavenly oxygen.

Jesus, while Your kingdom is hidden like the world under the sea, help me seek it and breathe in all my spirit needs to sustain me on earth.

CHOOSING YOUR BEACH PLAYLIST

My heart, O God, is steadfast . . . I will sing and make music.

PSALM 57:7 NIV

From mixtapes to CDs, and now to online apps, we have many means for picking and storing the perfect songs for a beach playlist. Playlist contents can range greatly depending on musical tastes, and the songs we choose beforehand will determine the soundtrack of our day.

Upbeat summer tunes will lift our spirits and give us energy to run around and play games and chat with friends on the beach. Softer, more relaxing songs may mellow us out and give us thoughtful rest under the sun as we lie on towels or sit under an umbrella, watching waves and walkers in a reverie. The songs we choose back at home help determine the disposition of our day.

In everyday life, hard times might tempt us to change our songs to complaints with more depressing melodies. These are the times we need to have a playlist ready, one picked out beforehand with songs of praise.

On earth, this lifetime is our only chance to sing songs of praise during trials. This kind of sacrifice is the sweetest, most genuine act of our will to love and honor God no matter what. It forms a deep and lovely bond with Jesus, who knows suffering better than anyone. We can choose for our life playlists songs of praise that say Jesus is worthy of worship even when our lives aren't sunny, making our communion with Him sweeter than the loveliest of beach days.

Jesus, remind me of Your cross. In my own moments of suffering, prepare in me a steadfast heart that sings worship to God.

BONFIRES ON THE BEACH

*"Why are you troubled, and why do doubts rise in your
minds? Look at my hands and my feet."*

LUKE 24:38–39 NIV

As the cool of the evening falls at sunset, a bonfire on the beach creates an atmosphere of calm camaraderie for those gathered around it. Smoke rises to the sky like incense, and the aroma of roasting wood and salty air is like a scented candle that sets the mood for healing conversations. When you are surrounded by your most loyal friends, these ideal moments are like therapy that soothes and softens hearts. This allows a deeper ache to surface that says, *This is how the world is supposed to be: good, beautiful, and lived with loved ones.*

We all have memories, if we are old enough, that have caused this view of a lovely world to dim. Maybe it's a loved one gone too soon, or a broken dream that causes you to doubt your identity. We all face events that cause us to question our belief in a loving God who promises all will be well. We wonder how we can trust Him when He allowed this to happen.

Jesus answers, "Look at my hands and my feet." There we see the marks of real love, where nails pierced Him. As real as our pain is, His love is *realer*, and He is the soother of our pain and sorrows. Jesus urges us not to be troubled, because He proved His goodness on the cross, and the incense of His perfect sacrifice always rises to God. Like the warmth of a bonfire promising healing and relief, He welcomes us to share our heart struggles with Him.

*Jesus, I ache for Your goodness and reassurance. Remind
me that You are making all things right again.*

ANCHOR DECOR

We have this hope as an anchor for the soul, firm and secure.

HEBREWS 6:19 NIV

B each homes often feature nautical decor such as the anchor. The anchor represents, among other things, the ability to explore ocean wonders while remaining safely grounded, especially when storms arise. No matter the time or tide, the heavy, hooked iron secures our spot.

If a simple beach decoration can serve to remind us of safety and security, what do we decorate our lives with? How about mementos of the times in our lives when God revealed Himself as a present help and dependable Father? These testimonies dig our anchors further into the secure promises of God.

We need reminders of these instances because we can easily forget how faithful God is. Maybe He provided rent. Maybe He sustained a family member through an illness. It can be helpful to mark those times when God has proven trustworthy, and perhaps certain images–anchors, pictures, Bible verses, a stone, a flower–remind us of God's goodness. Placing this kind of decoration in view reminds us of God's dependability in present storms when they threaten to overshadow past testimonies.

When the waves rise and hard times roll in with strong currents, remembering God's faithfulness will help keep our anchors secure. When the brighter days come, we can add to the decor of our lives another reminder of God's trustworthiness and goodness.

God, mark my memory with times You've been true and kind to me so that my trust runs deep, like an anchor in the sea.

BEACHES AND BEDS:
TALKING WITH GOD

Thus the LORD used to speak to Moses face to face, as a man speaks to his friend.

EXODUS 33:11 ESV

In the Old Testament, God talked to people in mysterious ways, often using a visual accompaniment, like a cloud of smoke or a burning bush. In the New Testament, God came even closer as a man, and in Jesus He calls us friends (John 15:15); we can speak to Him now as we do to a trusted confidant. Yet today we may still associate certain natural areas with the presence of God, and for many this is the beach. The greatness of the ocean and expanse of the sky recall images of heaven; surely if God is anywhere on earth, the beach is big and beautiful enough for Him.

As you turn your gaze up toward the enormity of the sky, with thoughts of how big, awesome, and indescribably holy and wondrous He is, you remember that He chooses to converse with you here, like a familiar friend.

Any chance to get away in nature helps redirect our focus toward the face of our truest Companion. The truth is, though, God is not any more present at the beach or in nature than He is in every space we inhabit. We always have access to Him, whether on the beach or in our beds. The same God who is powerful enough to create scenes of oceanic masterpieces is present wherever we are.

God, thank You for Your constant companionship.
Help me stay connected to You wherever I am.

WATCHING FOR LIGHTNING

Be strong, and let your heart take courage; wait for the LORD!

PSALM 27:14 ESV

I t cuts across a darkened sky above a beach horizon, branching out in brilliant white-hot streaks. Whether or not raindrops are falling, you cannot predict the exact moment it will strike. It foreshadows thunder, and is itself as unpredictable as the sporadic electricity dancing in the clouds. Lightning lights up the night only under the supervision and conduction of Providence.

When we have to wait for God to show up or come through for us, it may already be raining and storming on our plans, or there might be a lull, as if nothing exciting or life-bringing will happen again. When the trajectory of our lives seems dull or bleak, we might wish that receiving God's promises were as easy and immediate as turning on a lamp or flipping a light switch. But God's promises and His plans for coming through for us are more like the unpredictable ways of lightning.

We may not know exactly when, where, or how it will take place, but when God comes through, He lights up the night sky and brightens our lives right at the opportune moment. We are called to wait and watch the sky, holding strength and courage in our hearts. God is always on the move, and His plans are as strong and pointed as lightning bolts over the beach.

Father, help me wait expectedly for Your plans
and promises to brighten my world.

SAVORY BEACH BRUNCH

*"You are the salt of the earth, but if salt has lost its
taste, how shall its saltiness be restored?"*

MATTHEW 5:13 ESV

W hen you are sleeping soundly in your soft beach-house bed, lightly swaddled in blankets with your head sunk into a plush pillow, it is glorious to know you can sleep in. You've already slept past breakfast time, but what's that smell wafting into your room? You pop up out of the bedcovers, your nose directed upward. Bacon! Someone is cooking brunch. And the beautiful thing about brunch is you can sleep in and have your bacon too.

You throw off the bedsheets and rise with a grin. In the kitchen, eggs are being scrambled, avocados and heirloom tomatoes are being sliced while the bacon is sizzling in a pan. You pour some coffee and bless the bacon-bearing hands preparing the meal and help set the table on the porch.

The savory brunch spread on the balcony is salty and scrumptious. The salt makes the flavors pop and melt in your mouth. You are wide-awake now and ready for what the day has in store.

Jesus calls us the salt of the earth; we add the flavor of God to the world. Many are still asleep to the goodness and the life of God, which is better than anything. (Yes, even bacon.) Our saltiness, or the truth we carry in Jesus, wakes people from their slumber; the aroma of Christ is worth getting up for. When we abide in Christ, keeping our saltiness, the world wakes up.

*Jesus, let Your presence be tangible in me so I
help rouse a slumbering world to life in You.*

A RACE FOR THE KEYS

"I will give you the keys of the kingdom of heaven."

MATTHEW 16:19 ESV

The journey to a long-awaited beach-house vacation often includes patient sitting, restroom stops, meal breaks, snacks, more restroom stops, laughter, and embarrassing singalongs initiated by parents. When the crew finally arrives at the beach home, everyone scrambles and pleads for the honor of opening the door. Holding the keys is like holding authority and a great responsibility to open the beach home with the rest, relaxation, and heavenly joy it promises for family life that week.

If the kingdom of God is like a beach-house destination, and Jesus tells us He has given us, His followers and friends, the keys, it should spark joy and passion in our hearts that we share in the authority of bringing heaven to earth. What we do and say on earth holds eternal weight and consequence.

Many of us may want to hand the keys back. We don't trust ourselves to know enough, to be responsible or selfless enough, to lead others to the kingdom. But Jesus promises never to leave or forsake us. He is the Head of the household, or the church, and the responsibilities He gives us on earth only remind us how much we need to lean on Him and incline our ears to His counsel.

When He hands you an unexpected key in your life to open His kingdom to someone you know, race to the door and unlock it. For many it will be like a first-time arrival at a home in paradise, and you get the joy of ushering him or her in.

Jesus, I'm amazed You trust me with the keys to Your kingdom.
Show me the people in my life I can usher toward the door.

SLIPPERY SEAWEED

*It is my prayer that your love may abound more and more, with knowledge
and all discernment, so that you may approve what is excellent.*

Some ocean water is crystal clear, like a glass surface that allows full sight of the ocean floor. These waters occur usually in more tropical, exotic locations. But often on the coasts of the United States the ocean water is murkier and darker, mysteriously hiding what's underneath. Seaweed can be an unpleasant surprise when you go swimming, if it unexpectedly entangles you in its slimy trap.

Sin is as undesirable as slippery seaweed as it tries to catch us and keep us from God's good gifts. It's much easier to swim unhindered by seaweed when the water is pristine; but when it isn't, God helps us by placing more excellent options in our lives, like true companionship, rich literature and soulful art, opportunities to view nature, or the simple pleasures of cooking together and serving one another in the day to day. These privileges shine a godly light even in murky waters.

Swimming in the ocean is not about avoiding seaweed; it's about having fun, basking in God's creation and recreation with pals. In the same way, life following God is not only about avoiding sins; it's about enjoying Him and each other. Focusing on what's good, approving what is excellent, and pursuing those things help clear the "water" in which we swim in life, we will avoid the seaweed with greater clarity and discernment.

*God, clarify what is like seaweed for me, and help me swim
unhindered toward what is most beneficial and beautiful in life.*

PIERS TO HEAVENLY OUTLOOKS

Whatever is true, whatever is honorable, whatever is just, whatever is pure,
whatever is lovely, whatever is commendable . . . think about these things.

PHILIPPIANS 4:8 ESV

Pillars, sturdy and built to withstand the waves, are placed in parallel pairs out from the shore into the ocean, holding up a platform that is also a pier. If you stand on the end of a pier at sunrise or sunset, you'll see a view in which the veil between earth and heaven seems sheer: water without end and sky without limit.

Our thoughts are like mind bridges, or piers, leading toward different destinations of attitudes and outlooks. Each thought can lead our minds, hearts, and emotions in many directions. For example, thinking about what others have and we don't can lead to self-pity and envy. Envy is an uncomfortable destination. On the other hand, thoughts of what we do have, of how God has provided for us, can lead us to gratitude and contentment. Thoughts about times when someone betrayed us lead to loneliness, isolation, and unrelenting hurt. But choosing to forgive and focus on why you love that person will free your heart and guide your mind toward peace and unity.

Pay careful attention to where you are guiding your interior pier pillars. You have the ability to direct your thought bridges to heavenly views. Center your thoughts on what is lovely, just, pure, and good–"Whatever is commendable." Setting your "pier" toward God makes the veil to heaven thinner and will bring you to a view of peace and serenity.

Father, help me build a walkway that leads
people to divine views of Your goodness.

JUMPING WAVES

Though one may be overpowered, two can defend themselves.
A cord of three strands is not quickly broken.

ECCLESIASTES 4:12 NIV

There are different playful techniques for how to take on the waves when you are out in the ocean with friends. You can let yourself float like a human surfboard, riding up and down at the will of the wave. Or you can dive or flip through each wave that comes, cutting through the rushing water hands first and emerging on the other side feeling like an aquatic acrobat. Perhaps the most common way to encounter waves is to jump over them, rising above and moving through by the force of your feet kicking off the ocean floor.

Sometimes the waves are too strong; they can cut your jump short and knock you over. But if you join hands with your friends, forming a line, when the stronger waves come and you jump together, the combined force and strength of the line can withstand much stronger waves.

Many times we can try to look at the waves or obstacles in our lives as challenges to take on and handle to the best of our ability. But often the bigger problems are too big and strong for us to handle alone. Grabbing hands with friends and family and forming a line or partnership allow us to jump even bigger waves and get through to the other side triumphant. Waves are fun to play in; problems are not. Keep some friends handy so you can support each other, both in the ocean and out.

God, remind me to join forces with others when forbidding waves confront me. Show me whom I can support at the same time.

HOPE FLOATIES

*Hope does not put us to shame, because God's love has been
poured into our hearts through the Holy Spirit.*

ROMANS 5:5 NIV

Children with their slender arms swallowed by big, neon-colored floaties
are cute when they bob in the ocean. Now imagine an adult or even a
teenager wearing floaties. That would be an odd sight to behold! Floaties: cute
on kids, silly on adults.

Like floaties, hope is more commonly associated with children. If they
haven't faced many trials or hardships yet, children are natural hopers. They
find it easy to dream up good things for themselves and the world in general.
On the other hand, hope in adults can seem naive. We get the impression, as we
grow up, that hope is just wishful thinking. Hope in a good God? And heaven
with our own rooms and Jesus' specific love for each of us? Those are things of
children's stories–or are they?

The Bible has something different to say about hope. It says that we rejoice
in difficulty and sufferings because they produce character that leads to hope
(Romans 5:3-4). Rather than being naive, hope is actually a side of maturity:
through tough times we learn that no matter what happens on earth, our hope
in Christ will not put us to shame. Our salvation is sure, God's love secure, and
we can hope in Him without fear of disappointment.

While we outgrow floaties, we never outgrow hope. We grow into it in fuller
measure.

*Jesus, when I need Your hope to keep me afloat in
life, help me carry my belief in You bravely.*

THE PERFECT WAVE

The Lord is not slow to fulfill his promise as some count slowness, but is patient toward you, not wishing that any should perish, but that all should reach repentance.

2 PETER 3:9 ESV

Inexperienced surfers may watch professionals out in the water, lying on their surfboards and letting wave after wave go by. *Why didn't he take that one? It looked ideal for a great surf. Surely he missed out on that one.*

Then the surfer-pro starts to paddle with his hands and positions his surfboard. The perfect wave has come, and he rides it in powerfully and with such grace that the bystanders stand in awe, gaping at the skill and timing on display.

Of course, professional surfers know how to judge the status of the wind and the water so they know the right time to take a wave. Regular beach visitors lack the skills and experience to gauge these things.

In the same way, we might look around us at the status of the world and think, *Jesus, right about now would be a good time for You to come back.* We complain, maybe even challenge God, saying He is late or failing to keep His promise.

But God gauges the conditions better than anyone. He knows the right time to bring on the new creation and wipe away every tear. He patiently waits so all have the chance to be saved. Our role is to pray, trust, and spread the gospel, because as sure as the waves roll in every day, Jesus is coming back. He might not ride in on a wave, but we can rest on the guarantee–He will come at the perfect time.

Jesus, give me patience and trust to wait for You faithfully.

SAND VOLLEYBALL

You are the body of Christ, and each one of you is a part of it.

1 CORINTHIANS 12:27 NIV

The sky is cloudless, and the sand volleyball court is lit up by the sun like a stage awaiting its players. A game has been proposed, and the teams are starting to form; players spread out to fill positions. Some are gifted in bumping and digging, others are great at setting, and then you split up the powerful spikers. The participants migrate to their team's side of the net, and the volley begins.

The white ball skyrockets with each contact back and forth, soaring over the net with the players moving underneath, following its every move. The best teams interact smoothly, and the setter calls the plays. If the team members practice enough and work together, they will be unstoppable. They will move around the sand court as if they are dancing. It's awesome to watch.

That team spirit applies to our work as the body of Christ. If we honor each other's giftings—each important for the benefit of the whole—and are united, synchronized in our efforts for the kingdom, the world watches in awe and God is glorified. When we don't compete among ourselves, we can focus on maintaining a bond of peace. We then compete against only the enemy of God and work together in Christ's victory, as in sync as a winning volleyball team. Then the church is unstoppable, a sight to behold.

*God, thank You for the role I have to play in Your
church; help me mesh smoothly with my "team."*

BEACH BAG READY

The hour has come for you to wake from sleep. For salvation
is nearer to us now than when we first believed.

ROMANS 13:11 ESV

How satisfying it is to wake up in the morning knowing that your beach bag is already packed and ready to go. You can look forward to all the day ahead has to offer: the yellow sunshine, warm sand under your feet, cool, refreshing waves–a taste of paradise on earth. It's even better if you packed light so that you're not hauling a bulging bag with clunky beach accessories. The beach itself and the company you keep are the main attractions, not the stuff you take with you.

Our entrance into God's kingdom will be like waking up to a bright beach morning, only we don't know when it will occur. Yet we are told to always be ready. How do we prepare for such an adventure and beautiful dawn, no longer a taste, but here in fullness, paradise unveiled in reality? We pack light.

We won't be carrying any of our bulky material goods with us to this eternal shore. We can prepare our "bags" with simple acts of love and devotion, but the fact is, all we need will be there already. When we truly awake for the first time to explore the kingdom, a landscape of perfection, indestructible and filled with the light of God's presence, let's be ready to go! Let's lay aside heavy, useless worldly goods and hold on to what matters–hearts completely devoted to Jesus and acts of service for His pleasure.

Father, as I live and serve You, let my life be full
of acts of love to present to King Jesus.

BOARDWALK CHOICES

I have set the LORD always before me; because he is
at my right hand, I shall not be shaken.

B each boardwalks are pathways of provision–meal choices, beach acces-
sory stores, refreshing beverages, and dessert stops–yet overwhelming in
their numerous options. Any little child could be easily shaken by navigating the
crowd of strangers and not knowing what to choose. But that's what parents are
for, holding the child's hand and walking slowly and pointing out each option.
The child trusts the parent's direction and is comforted and calm enough to
choose.

We can be overwhelmed by choices: Should we try for this job, move, date
this person, buy this house, go to this university, invest in this opportunity,
have children now, start a new ministry? It seems the decisions never stop. It's
like a never-ending boardwalk with unlimited options. Anxiety can arise that we
might choose wrongly and miss out or fail in the direction we take.

God is like a good, wise, and insightful Parent at our side, holding our
hands and calmly reassuring us as He guides us through the crowds and the
choices. He is bigger than all the options and outcomes combined, and what
matters, what we want most, is the Lord Himself. If we enjoy His company, rely
on His steadying hand and guidance, we'll find making choices can be as fun
and exciting as a stroll on a beach boardwalk.

God, when too many options bring stress and anxiety, remind me
that You are by my side and will give me wisdom to choose well.

THE GLORY OF STARFISH

Be imitators of God, as beloved children. And walk in love.

EPHESIANS 5:1–2 ESV

S tarfish are named for their likeness to the five-pointed-star drawings of our childhood. They are a treat to find on the beach because they are alive! We can feel the smooth or bumpy flesh of their arms and turn them over to watch the little motor tubules on their undersides move about. After just a moment or so, though, we can gently return them to the sea, where they're able to breathe and continue living. Starfish may not shine and sparkle as actual stars do in the nighttime sky, but they move, eat, and live their God-ordained starry, fishy lives. It's an ordinary glory.

We may not be perfect examples of our heavenly Father just yet on earth, but we still look like Him. We may not be as spectacular as, say, the Sistine Chapel or other works of art depicting heavenly perfection. Yet we are not made of marble like Michelangelo's masterpiece, *David*. Sculptures of saints and other religious artworks can point to the beauty of spiritual things and heavenly beings, but we are not being transformed into the likeness of a statue or painting, but a real man, Jesus (2 Corinthians 3:18). He lived, walked, ate, and (most important) served perfectly in accordance with the will of God. He was and is an extraordinary glory.

He is making us like Him, with hearts of flesh, not stone. And our ability to live, move, breathe, act, and serve like Jesus is an ordinary glory that shines brighter than stars. We may feel like floppy starfish in our attempts to be like Jesus, but the point is we look like Him; we carry humanity and heaven inside because of Him. We are ordinarily glorious.

Father, as I embrace being human, set my eyes on Jesus and fashion my heart after His.

WHALE WATCHING

*When the L*ORD *restored the fortunes of Zion, we were like those who dream.*
Then our mouth was filled with laughter, and our tongue with shouts of joy.

Whales are the joyous, gentle giants of the ocean, and we love to watch them swim, powerfully glide, and even breach the water and spin in the air, coming back down with a glorious splash. We also love to listen to them. Their baritone calls and rumbling vocals can sometimes resemble the deepest belly laugh on the planet. When they call to one another, speaking their secret language across quiet ocean waters, it is mysterious and powerfully profound, a symphony of sounds in accordance with the joy of their existence.

Joy is not so much emotion, like happiness; it is actually listed among the fruits of the Spirit (Galatians 5:22). Joy fills. Like water spilling into a whale's open mouth, filling up the gigantic cavity and rushing down to the whale's belly, joy fills emptiness and bubbles back up in laughter.

When souls thirsty for God's presence come together and begin to worship, joy comes in and fills everyone to capacity. Songs of heavenly praise and worship resound, a symphony to God. This kind of unity and love experienced on earth is like a dream. Our hearts call to one another and to God.

Like the whales, we share a certain language that belongs to those who are spiritual, who have looked upon Jesus and been emptied of the world in order to be filled with His joy. It is soul speak. God created us to be filled with His joy like the belly-laughing whales.

God, pour out Your joy on Your people. Make Your church
sound like heaven with beautiful songs and great laughter.